Storage Area Network Administrator, Storage Architect, SAN Storage En...
Interview Bottom Line Practical Questions, Answers and advice for acing a SAN Storage job interview

Preface:
A note from the publisher:
Why this book:
It will remind you of key SAN Questions
Storage Area Networks tricks, tips, facts just in time
Perfect answers to get hired for any SAN Jobs
Successful fibre channel SAN, NAS, Job Interview
Start & Close any SAN Storage Job Interview Successfully

Intended audience:
This is intended for anyone who is attending a SAN job interview.
Complete vendor neutral SAN Storage Interview answers for the following Jobs:
Storage Specialist, SAN Engineer, SAN Administrator, SAN Systems Administrator, Storage Administrator, SAN Storage Engineer, Storage Architect, Storage Manager , Storage Professional

It will help you to convey powerful and useful SAN storage information to the employer successfully. There is no information available that connects all the dots for a SAN job interview, for the benefit of all author is sharing his personal interview notes, unique ideas, accumulated experience & observations of years of SAN, why reinvent the wheel when you can learn from people who have who have already figured things out.
Storage Area Networks (SANs) have become one of the hottest skills. It's our observation that many of these questions are also used by recruiters and hiring managers for SAN staff augmentation.
It has been well written to make it a very quick read. Practicing with this interview questions and answers in the mirror will help with your replies to questions and pass with flying colors. Try to be in parking lot an hour before the interview and use this time to read over this e-book it covers technical, non-technical, HR and Personnel questions.
Just in time interview preparation in as low as 60 minutes.
You will learn to practice mock interviews for a storage professional position.
Interview Questions and Suggested Answers related to the following and more:
All the aspects of SAN Administration
Multiple enterprise storage vendors
All Flash and hybrid storage arrays
Administration and troubleshooting of flash arrays
Manage, Maintain and Develop Storage Infrastructure
Business Continuity Concepts
Local and Remote Replication
Storage Virtualization Technologies
Enterprise Storage Systems
Microcode Upgrades, Switch Configuration
Connectivity, Zoning, ISL, Windows, Solaris, Linux, UNIX
Mapping, Masking, Storage Configuration
Storage Integration in Heterogeneous Environment
Best Practices Standards for System Performance and Stability
Disaster Recovery and Business Continuity

Configure and administer SAN/NAS
Monitor and manage SAN space and I/O utilization
Fibre Channel SANs infrastructures
Maintain disk Storage Arrays
RAID Implementations, Pool Storage Design
LUN Sizing and Volume Configuration
Fibre attached & ISCSI-based storage devices
Managing a SAN switching fabric
Snapshot technologies
Updating and maintaining SAN connected servers
Virtual tape and physical tape libraries
Data de-duplication
Data Migration
SAN Switches and Fabric
Storage Virtualization
Storage Management
Data Management
Continuity Management
Fiber Channels for SAN
Why Fiber Channel, SAS
FC Layers & Related Components
FC Topologies, Terminology & Addressing
Application Analysis Questions
Best Practices Questions
CIFS Questions
Continuity Management Questions
Data Management Questions
Data Protection Questions
Deduplication Questions
Design and Implementation Questions
Direct Attached Storage Questions
Disaster Recovery Questions
DR Questions
Dynamic Tiering Questions
Encryption Questions
FC Layers & Related Components Questions
FC Questions
FC Topologies, Terminology & Addressing Questions
FCIP, Ifcp, Ficon Questions
Fibre Channel Fabric Questions
Fibre Channel Packet Design Questions
Fibre Channel Protocol (FCP) Questions
Fibre Channel Switches Questions
Fibre Channel Topologies Questions
Fibre Channel Zoning Questions
Fibre Channels for SAN Questions
Global Sparing Questions

HBA's For FCP and Iscsi Questions
High Availability Questions
Hosts, Host Bus Adapters Questions
iscsi SAN Design Questions
Links Questions
Main Components Questions
Multi-Path Software Questions
NAS and SAN Questions
Network Attached Storage Questions
NFS Questions
Protocols Questions
Problem Resolution Questions
RAID Questions
Replication and Mirror Questions
SAN Based Backup Questions
SAN Command Line Tools Questions
SAN Design Questions
SAN Fabric Management Questions
SAN Standard Operating Procedures Questions
SAN Storage Pool Questions
SAS Questions
SCSI Commands and Versions Questions
SCSI Via IP (Iscsi) Questions
Small Computer System Interface (SCSI) Questions
Snapshots, Snap mirror, Snap restore Questions
Storage Area Networks Questions
Storage Array Data Encryption
Storage Management Questions
Storage Need Questions
Storage Resources Design Questions
Storage Virtualization Questions
Tape less Backup Questions
TCP/IP Encapsulated SCSI Questions
NDMP Backup Questions
Topology Design Questions
Vendor Solutions Questions
Volume Management Questions
Replication Questions
Thin Provisioning Questions
Tiering Questions
Performance tuning Questions
Disaster recovery Questions
Direct Attached Storage
Network Attached Storage
Storage Area Networks

Good luck on your Interview.

Buy with Confidence (Read sample before you buy the book...)

Reviews/Feedback:
Please tell how this book helped you prepare for SAN job interview by using "Share your thoughts with other customers" icon

INDEX

Bottom Line Job interview?

Interview question

As a SAN administrator how will you tell your boss how many drives are required for a requirement?

How to calculate HDD capacity?

You need to provision SAN storage with a certain IOPS.

How will you find what kind of disks you need?

How will you calculate Max IOPS an HBA Port can generate to any LUN?

What is Q-Depth? How to calculate it?

How will you calculate number of drives required?

If you know I/O load and IOPS, how will you calculate how many drives will be needed?

How will you calculate HDD Capacity?

What is relation between rotational speed and latency time?

What SAN design you will choose? Why?

What are multi-pathing schemes and which one to use for optimal performance?

With Active- Passive storage array what multipathing policy you will choose?

Tell us a generic method to provision SAN Storage from any Array?

How will you discover SAN disks on Hosts?

How will you get the WWN of all your HBA's to provision SAN storage?

How will you find errors on various OS operating systems to troubleshoot problems?

For troubleshooting have you collected logs from a SAN Switch?

What is Buffer-to-Buffer Credits?

How will you calculate Number of Buffers required?

Which load balancing policies are used between Inter Switch Links? Explain with an example?

What best practices you will follow to setup ISL Trunking?

How will you decide how many storage arrays can be attached to a single host?

What is Drooping? How to check it?

What Factors you will consider for designing a SAN?

Explain your experience with disk sparing?

Explain Brocade VCS Fabric technology?

Name a product for Ethernet Data Center Bridging (DCB)?

What is the difference between multimode and single mode fibre?

How to trouble shoot a fibre optic signal?

Can you allocate a LUN larger than 2.19TB limit of MBR ?

How can you see the Load on the open systems connected to SAN?

How will you calculate IOPS per drive?

How to calculate RPMs of SSD?

How will you calculate the required band width with write operations?

How will you calculate Raw Capacity?

How do you know what type of fibre cable is needed?

Explain the Device Masking Architecture in storage arrays?

Explain SAN zoning?

What is the difference between Hard and Soft Zoning?

What is Port Zoning?

What is WWN zoning?

What is LUN, Logical Unit Number?

What is LUN masking?

Why we need LUN Masking?

How all switches and directors in the fabric maintain the same zoning information?

Explain NPIV?

Why you will use N-Port Virtualization?

How will you ensure that SAN-attached tape devices are represented consistently in a host operating system?

Have you used CLI to create Zones on a SAN switch?

Explain your experience of SAN switch firmware update via CLI?

Explain your experience in managing SAN switch ports via CLI?

What are the types of IOPS?

What is the Small block random I/O for various disk types?

Explain your experience with Offloaded Data Transfer (ODX)?

How will you backup large amount of data on heterogeneous network attached storage? How to set it up?

What is a Multimode Fibre Cable?

Where you encrypt Data Stored in SAN?

Explain your experience with Data Deduplication?

Have you used short stroking?

Explain N Port virtualization? Which switch supports NPV?

How to use SAN over long distance?

Explain various connectivity options for long distance replication?

What factors affect IOPS?

How will you calculate the maximum number of concurrent I/O requests on AIX?

How can I use exit status in UNIX to see if a command ran successfully?

Which Commands you can use in UNIX for Data Migration?

What type of connectors are 10G SFP modules?

Explain the types of fibre optic cable connectors?

What are the different types of fibre optic cable based on fibre types?

Explain specifications of Mode Conditioning Fiber Optic Cables?

In Storage area networks speed of various components currently you have?

Where have you used GBIC? What you do if GBIC fails?

What is SFP?

What is SAS?

Dust particles and contamination cause signal loss across fiber optic connectors, which guidelines you will follow for connector inspection and cleaning?

Have you used Disk Write Patrol in SAN?

Explain Thick Provision Lazy Zeroed Virtual disk?

Which types of virtual disks you have used?

What are the various types of LUN Volumes?

How will you Transfer a file using network?

How will you Remove Cores on UNIX?

Explain iSCSI naming conventions?

What are some of the best practices for SAN Designing?

What is the fan-out ratio?

What is the expansion fan-in ratio?

How will you calculate ISL oversubscription?

On UNIX systems how will you remove a hung process?

Explain the I/O Data Path in a SAN?

Explain the role of Fibre channel layers?

When you will use VLAN Tagging?

Which HBA you recommend? Why?

What flag you will set when sharing director ports between hosts with multiple vendor operating systems? How?

Explain TCQ?

Explain CRC?

As a SAN administrator you need to schedule a job on UNIX? What command you can use?

Explain Credit?

What are the components of HBA drivers?

Have you replaced a HBA?

Which specifications you check for HDD reliability?

Why you use switched fabric?

On a Microsoft Windows Server you are unable to initialize master boot record (MBR) disks and you get error message "the disk is write protected ". What can you do?

You need to reclaim free space while migrating from a Thick to a Thin Volume. Can you use UNIX utilities such as migratepv?

Explain your experience with SAN Topologies

Name the main types of storage network components?

Which Cloud service is related with Storage?

Explain the concept of Frames in SAN?

How will you find HBA's on AIX?

How will you find HBA's on ESxi?

How will you check the RAID table for corruption in LINUX?

Have you used Traffic Isolation Zoning?

How you make your SAN ready for heterogeneous switches?

Can you migrate to a new SAN Switch without downtime?

Give a generic high level method to setup ISCSI

Give a generic high level method to setup replication

What is a World Wide Name (WWN)?

What are the classes of attacks against SANs?

What is FCAP (Fibre Channel Authentication Protocol)?

Why the actual size of disk is less than logical size?

Explain various connectivity options for long distance?

Explain PID Port Identifier Format ?

What are the various components of WWWN?

How to find Peak Rolling Average (PRA) in SAN?

What are SAN 24-Bit Port Address Fields?

What are all the SHARE Recovery Tiers?

How will you define various systems availability?

Explain ROI, RTO and RPO?

How will you be replicating a database so that it may be easier to restore?

Why you use block level storage systems?

What Buffer to Buffer Credits for Long Distances you recommend?

What kind of SAN deployments have you done?

Can you explain the structure and organization of FC Data?

Explain how you do block level storage virtualization?

What you like about storage virtualization?

Explain the use of Datagram

How does FSPF work?

What can you do to fix zoning information in FibreZone database?

Explain the difference between "In-Band" and "Out-of-Band" Virtualization?

What kind of disks you recommend for various types of data?

Explain the Structure of Storage department and roles and responsibilities?

What type of fabric mode you must set your switches to?

How you Discover device names of LUNs on an HP-UX server?

How will you calculate raw capacity?

What is a Meta Device?

What is used for Device Masking?

You are a SAN Admin and Users are complaining about performance how can you see the performance statistics?

What is an HBA?

What are the ways to manage Brocade switch?

Explain Fibre Channel logins?

What information is passed during PLOGI?

What information is passed during PRLI?

Explain FLOGI?

What you use to avoid storage device corruption in vCenter Server?

Explain fabric merge? How to do it?

You got a failed fibre switch what actions you will take?

How will you secure a fibre switch management?

Explain your experience with dynamic disk

To perform disk management tasks in Windows Server 2008?

Is it possible to setup an ISL between Cisco and Brocade switches?

Explain your experience with disk duplexing

Explain your experience with logical unit number (LUN)

Explain your experience with VDS hardware provider?

What is use of Fibre Channel Link Services?

Fibre Channel is an American National Standards Institute (ANSI) interface that acts as a general transport vehicle to simultaneously deliver the command sets of which protocols?

What Replication Modes you are familiar with?

How you manage Fiber Channel?

What transmission you will use to fully utilize available bandwidth?

Explain the use of ordered sets?

Explain CIM and SMI-S

How many parts CIM have?

A user wants to access block-oriented and file based disks of the same storage system, what can you do?

Explain ASIC?

Explain FPGA?

Which port is used by the SAN (Storage Area Network) incorporating SCSI drivers without the need of attaching extra disks?

What is RDM? What kind of LUN you need for RDM?

How do you view SAN disks using Logical Volume Management?

What you need for Brocade switches to login?

Tell us SAN Design Lifecycle?

How to perform performance analysis in a SAN Environment?

What Methods have you used to improve cache performance?

Give some examples of HBAs?

Explain Fibre Channel Protocols?

Name Basic SAN Components?

How to update Linux OS when you install a new hardware such as HBA?

How will you allow LINUX to see more than 0 LUNs?

Explain Fibre Channel technology options nomenclature   100-SM-LL-L?

What are different SAN Topologies?

Explain different Fibre Channel Ports?

What is World Wide Name (WWN)?

What is Inter-Switch Link (ISL)?

What is ISL Trunking?

Do you know Zoning Best Practices?

Name Basic SAN Components?

Define Replication?

Explain how will you perform replication for HDS arrays?

What Types of Configuration are possible with Replication?

Explain how will you setup HUR Replication?

How will you identify and find a command device in Hitachi SAN?

How will you manage HDS Array replication by using CLI?

Explain Inflow Control?

Explain what is the various Volume statuses in HDS replication?

Name Hitachi HDS storage array which supports virtualization?

Explain the architecture of HDS VSP array?

How will you monitor HDS, Hitachi Storage Arrays?

Explain the functions of SVP?

What is HDT?

Explain the use of HDP?

When will you use CLPR?

When will you enable Port Security?

How will you prevent illegal access of a LUN, when sharing?

What is a FAN in Ratio?

Which protocol is used in windows to share file?

iSCSI naming uses which service?

Users complain about slow file transfers on a SUN server with an Emulex HBA. How to check the settings of the HBA?

Which file control the ability on a Sun Solaris host to see the disks?

What is sd.conf?

How to add a disk to a Sun Solaris host online?

How to view disk usage in UNIX?

What is the 64-bit hardware address for a Fibre Channel HBA?

Name a few Cisco MDS 9000 products?

Which MDS-9000 director is capable of supporting the emerging 10 Gb bandwidth?

Which native command on a B-series switch provides data for troubleshooting?

What unique ID is assigned to a SAN Switch?

Explain the difference between initiator-based and mutual CHAP authentication?

What is LUN Trespass?

What are the CHAP security levels?

How to discover newly added LUNs on HP-UX?

Explain SAN Virtualization?

How to force the host to perform a Fabric login to a switch in an Emulex HBA Solaris host installation?

FC_AL tape drive to a fibre channel switch was connected.

How the switches identify the drive, during FLOGI?

How to mount and assign the LUN On the HP-UX Backup server?

What are the options in Iputil?

What is HBAnywhere?

Define Some Media Protection-RAIDs that can be configured?

What are the advantages of using a RAID-10? When to use?

What is Dynamic Sparing?

How you discover LUNs on AIX?

How to discover new disks on Linux?

How to extend a file system on Linux?

How to extend an uncounted ReiserFS file system?

If a SUN Host cannot see disks, what can you do?

You assigned LUNs from a Storage array and Veritas volume manager on a host sees too many LUNs or ghost LUNs, what could be the reason?

Explain IPC and Semaphores? How you can tune system?

What is iSCSI?

Explain various components of iSCSI?

iSCSI targets do not reconnect after a reboot. How to fix it?

What best practices you will follow for iSCSI?

What is your opinion about FCOE?

Why will you use Fibre Channel over Ethernet (FCoE)?

What is your observation about read and writes on SSDs?

Explain the use of WAN Optimization Controller (WOC)?

What is a Simplex volume?

What is OneFS?

Explain Consistency Groups?

A Drive letter which is on a SAN LUN, doesn't come back after a reboot of Microsoft Windows Server? How to fix it?

Name a Tier 1 Type Array?

Name a Tier 2 Type Array?

Name a Tier 3 Type of Storage Array?

What is twisted Pair Cable?

Why Fibre optic cables are used?

Is it possible to mix MultiMode 50 micon cables with MultiMode 62.5 micron cables?

Explain how to calculate Buffer Credit?

What switching components have you used storage network SAN?

Which File-Level Protocols you have used?

What is the use of GBIC?

For sequential reads and writes, which RAID is good?

What is SAN Storage virtualization?

What is thin provisioning?

What is a Dynamic Storage Pool?

What SAN Storage Array supports Dynamic Storage Pool?

What SAN topologies exist?

What is In-band?

What is Out-Of-Band?

What is a domain as it relates to a fabric?

What is FCID?

What is principal switch?

What is Core/Edge?

What type of switch you will use in the Edge tier?

What type of switch you will use in the Core?

What applications and IOs have you worked with?

Where should you keep log files?

What are the benefits of SAS?

Why RAID 5 not suitable for Data Base?

What types of Read and write operations are going on in a SAN Array?

Can you calculate IOPS?

Name long distance connectivity options?

How to find what kind of HBA is installed in AIX host?

How to find files in UNIX?

How will you scan for new disks which have been added to a tru64 host?

How To check status of tape and take the tapes offline, in UNIX?

Have you created LUNs?

Have you used a mechanism to discover Storage Array without requiring the in-band array connectivity to the host?

Explain your experience with infrastructure management software to monitor and analyze SANs. How to discover missing devices?

How you identify a Storage Array on SAN?

Have you used Locks in Storage Arrays? Examples?

Symmetrix External Locks

How you View Application Registrations on a Array?

Explain your experience with managing the Devices on an Array by Commands?

How to view Storage Capacities to Hosts?

How will you be verifying Network Services?

You found that you have a problem with one director. How you can check the config?

What products you have used to create duplication within a disk array?

Explain your experience with a snapshot provider and Windows Server and Dynamic Disk?

You got replication Link error? How you can check?

Explain WAFL: Write Anywhere File Layout?

How Device Level Data is maintained?

Tell us a generic method for SAN based replication?

How will you setup & modify RDF attribute from a device?

How can you get all the devices listed?

How you can find new devices?

Replication is failing. What you can do?

Explain some replication Component Commands?

Explain replication operation?

Explain some troubleshooting you can do for replication issues?

In EMC storage array-based replication product SRDF:

Explain Control Operations in a replication?

How can you create a remote synchronous copy of production file systems at a remote location in NAS?

Name a multi pathing software?

Have you managed multipathing via command line?

Yes. I have used Power path command CLI:

In a HDS Hitachi SAN how will you perform path failover, fail back, and automatic load balancing?

How to monitor and manage all replication systems in HDS SAN? How to verify Recovery Point Objective (RPO)?

How will you manage (Create Pool, Lun & Map) Hitachi storage systems?

Explain iSCSI naming conventions?

Name a product that can create a point in time snapshot?

Explain different methods of flushing in write cache?

You Presented SAN Storage on a HP-UX, How will you discover?

Name the component in Storage Array which is used to present device to host?

Define a replication product?

SRDF

For which component failure in DMX, Port Bypass card is used?

How will you add a SAN Storage based disk tape library to Solaris OS?

In a SAN with EMC storage how will you check if there is a bad disk?

How many mirrors are possible with STD device?

Which protocol is used in windows to share file?

How data is handled in a backup copy mirror establish?

Name the replication operation in which link is suspended between R1 and R2, Read and write enable on R1 , R2

What are the operations you have for the mode of data mover fail over?

How will you Ensure Fibre Channel Security?

How to troubleshoot SCSI Bus Resets?

How will you synchronize system times on multiple UNIX servers?

What Types of Configuration are possible with Replications?

I can answer this with regard to SRDF:

What Replication Modes you familiar with?

If data cannot be copied from the R1 to the R2 when consistency protection is enabled, what will happen?

Which hard drives currently you have used in your SAN?

Explain why a LUN is trespassed in a Array?

How to restore it?

In Clariion Storage Array:

What is the difference between Fan-Out and Fan-in?

Which platform you suggest for virtual applications with VMware and Hyper-V integration?

How to add one system to another?

To add one VNX system to another

You are unable to upgrade firmware on a SAN switch, what could be a reason?

Why should you upgrade Firmware and Drivers of HBA's?

Give an example of random I/O workloads?

Which HDD you have used in a Storage Array?

For optimal performance of a LUN accessed by Windows hosts what you suggest?

How will you keep track of invalid tracks in replication?

For Time Finder and SRDF:

Which enterprise SAN arrays you have used?

Which RAIDs you have used? Explain its specifications?

Why Writes on RAID are different?

How will you analyze network packets from NAS?

Why it's difficult to backup a replicated file system?

How can you backup a replicated file system?

You need a Large LUN but you can not create metaLUNs, what can you do?

Explain the use of fsck (File System Check) on SAN storage? What are fsck various phases?

In your SAN report you see high "ENC out" errors, why?

How to display speed of SAN switch port?

Explain the difference between Full duplex and Half duplex?

Which Seven Tiers of Disaster Recovery was originally defined by SHARE to help identify the various methods of recovering mission-critical computer systems as required supporting business continuity?

After a firmware load on a SAN switch a port where an AIX host is connected is showing not ready, how to fix it?

Does NDMP support file level deduplication?

How to view free space of disks in a Storage Array that are mapped to DA (disk) directors?

How will you find the volumes which are not mapped to a front end channel on the Storage Array?

How to find a failed disk on a Storage Array?

Which parameter will tell you if a write operation could be sent directly to cache?

Which performance indicator shows information about Writes pending?

You provisioned SAN Storage to an AIX host, which filesystem you recommend if the user needs a 10TB filesystem?

How will you make sure that AIX host is capable of running JFS2?

Have you used ODM in AIX?

Users of NAS device are complaining that NAS is very slow to transfer files, what can you check?

You have Continuous Data Replication but there is a need to change the data on destination. Is it possible?

You are using multipathing. What parameter you enable for path health checking?

Explain the use of SCSI Reservation?

Have you seen a negative consequence of SPC-2 SCSI?

How will you add a new Fibre switch to an active zone set?

Explain Zoning Structure?

What is the difference between Fiber Channel Nodes and ports?

How Nodes communicate?

A file system from NAS was exported to a Linux server but you can not NFS mount it. What can you do?

What is the difference between hard and soft mount?

You have setup NAS and you want to find out which clients have mounted NFS exports?

Have you used devices to communicate with Storage Array?

How will you bring an replication adapter online?

How will you Write-disable the local device in a replication?

How will you calculate correct number of Replication adapters?

What will you monitor in replication?

How can you verify the size of a veritas file system on UNIX?

Which filesystem supports NFS4 ACL's and how to create it?

In a SAN environment with replication when physical links goes offline and soon comes back online what will happen?

On AIX you have attached a LUN which is greater than 1TB, but you see many SC & SENSE Data errors on the host? Why?

Have you used Kernel-based Virtual Machine?

How will you improve disk I/O performance on a SAN connected LINUX Server?

How will you Unmount busy devices on UNIX?

How to List files in UNIX?

Have you worked as a SAN Administrator? What were your responsibilities?

Tell us most important commands, CLI to manage a Brocade SAN?

What specifications you check for HDD Performance?

What is the impact of evolving Ethernet speed on SAN?

What is the current speed of Fiber Channel products?

Name some Gen 6 Products?

Explain the use of Brocade UltraScale chassis connectivity?

Name some of the Flash Storage arrays?

Explain the main difference between FMD and SSD?

Explain the technology behind EMC XtremIO?

Explain how VMware Site Recovery Manager works?

What is SAN?

Why you use SAN?

Think about what you already learn and remember easily?

NonTechnical/ Personal/ HR interview: Complimentary

Bottom Line Job interview?

Interview Question?

What are your greatest strengths?

What are your greatest weaknesses?

Had you failed to do any work and regret?

Where do you see yourself five years from now?

How Will You Achieve Your Goals?

Why are you leaving Your Current position?

Why are you looking for a new job?

Why should I hire you?

Aren't you overqualified for this position?

Describe a Typical Work Week?

Are You Willing to Travel?

Describe the pace at which you work?

How Did You Handle Challenges?

How do you handle pressure? Stressful situations?

How Many Hours Do You Work?

Why are you the best person for the job?

What are you looking for in a position?

What do you know about our organization?

What are your short term goals?

What Salary are you looking for?

Tell me more about yourself.

Why did you leave your previous job?

What relevant experience do you have?

If your previous co-workers were here, what would they say about you?

Where else have you applied?

What motivates you to do a good job?

Are you good at working in a team?

Has anything ever irritated you about people you've worked with?

Is there anyone you just could not work with?

Tell me about any issues you've had with a previous boss.

Do you have any questions?

Why did you choose this career?

What did you learn from your last job experience?

Why is there a gap in your resume?

How do you keep current and informed about your job and the industries that you have worked in?

Tell me about a time when you had to plan and coordinate a project from start to finish?

What kinds of people do you have difficulties working with?

What do you want to be in 5 years?

Explain an Ideal career for you?

What are your job responsibilities?

What is your dream job?

What skills you have?

What sets you apart?

If the project not gone as planned what action you will take?

What you do if you are unable to meet deadlines?

Interpersonal skill?

Improve?

What do you feel has been your greatest work-related accomplishment?

Have you ever had to discipline a problem employee? If so, how did you handle it?

Why do you want this position?

Why are you the best person for this job?

What about Technical writing?

How versatile you are? Can you do other works?

How do you manage time?

How do you handle Conflicts?

What kind of supervisory skills you have?

Any Bad Situation you could not solve?

Anything else you want to say?

About the Author:

Bottom Line Job interview?

Bottom line: You will learn to answer any questions in such a way that you match your qualifications to the job requirements.

Interview question

Example response
Try to customize your answers to fit the requirements of the job you are interviewing for.

As a SAN administrator how will you tell your boss how many drives are required for a requirement?

I will use the formula:
Total Approximate Drives required = (RAID Group IOPS / (Hard Drive Type IOPS)) + Large Random I/O adjustment + Hot Spares + System Drives

How to calculate HDD capacity?

Capacity = Heads X Cylinders X Sectors X Block Size

You need to provision SAN storage with a certain IOPS.

How will you find what kind of disks you need?

Input/output operations per second (IOPS) is the measure of how many input/output operations a storage device can complete within one second.

IOPS is important for transaction-based applications.

IOPS performance is heavily dependent on the number and type of disk drives.

To calculate IOPS of a Hard disk drive:

$$IOPS = \frac{1}{(Average\ Latency) + (Average\ Seek\ Time)}$$

To calculate IOPS in a RAID:

(Total Workload IOPS * Percentage of workload that is read operations) + (Total Workload IOPS * Percentage of workload that is read operations * RAID IO Penalty)

How will you calculate Max IOPS an HBA Port can generate to any LUN?

Max IOPS an HBA Port can generate to any LUN = (Device Queue Depth per LUN * (1 / (Storage Latency in ms/1000)))

What is Q-Depth? How to calculate it?

The queue depth is the maximum number of commands that can be queued on the system at the same time.

Q is the Queue Depth =Execution Throttle= Maximum Number of simultaneous I/O for each LUN on a particular path to the Storage Port.
Calculation of the maximum queue depth: The queue depth is the number of I/O operations that can be run in parallel on a device.
Q = Storage Port Max Queue Depth / (I * L),
I is the number of initiators per storage port
L is the quantity of LUNs in the storage group.
T = P * q * L

T = Target Port Queue Depth
P = Paths connected to the target port
Q = Queue depth
L = number of LUN presented to the host through this port
Execution Throttle= (Maximum Storage Port Command Queue) / (Host Ports)

How will you calculate number of drives required?

Total Approximate Drives required = (RAID Group IOPS / (Hard Drive Type IOPS)) + Large Random I/O adjustment + Hot Spares + System Drives

If you know I/O load and IOPS, how will you calculate how many drives will be needed?

Total Approximate Drives = (RAID Group IOPS / (Hard Drive Type IOPS)) + Large Random I/O adjustment + Hot Spares + System Drives

How will you calculate HDD Capacity?

Capacity = Heads X Cylinders X Sectors X Block Size

What is relation between rotational speed and latency time?

The Rotational speed and latency time is related as follows:

Latency time = (1/((Rotational Speed in RPM)/60)) * 0.5 * 1000 milli seconds

Latency and RPM:

HDD

Spindle RPM	Average rotational latency [ms]
I. 7,200	4.17
II. 10,000	3.00
III. 15,000	2.00

What SAN design you will choose? Why?

Core-Edge

This design includes redundant paths between switches,
As the fabric has two or more "core" switches in the center of the fabric,
This interconnects a number of "edge" switches. Hosts,
Storage and other devices connect to the free ports on the edge switches, in some cases also connect directly to the core switch.
It makes the fabrics highly scalable, without disruption to service.
I consider Core-Edge the most versatile forms of SAN design.

Here a picture of Core-Edge Topology:

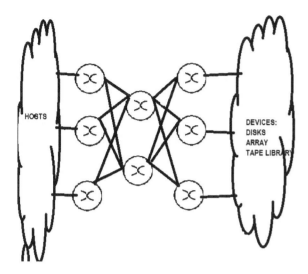

Benefits are: Higher ROI meets RTO, RPO & SLA and helps with consolidation, utilization of storage and ability to access any storage system from any host.
Core Edge Fabric Nomenclature: n1e*n2c*n3i
Where n1e= number of edge switches, n2c= number of core switches, n3i=number of ISL

What are multi-pathing schemes and which one to use for optimal performance?

Servers/ hosts uses multipathing for failover from one path to the other when one path from the Servers/host to the SAN becomes unavailable, the host switches to another path.
Servers/ hosts can also use multipathing for load balancing.

Types of policy:
1. Most Recently Used: The path used by a LUN is not be altered unless an event instructs the path to change. I will use this policy is for Active/Passive arrays and many pseudo active/active arrays. Most recently used (mru) selects the path most recently used to send I/O to a device.

2. Fixed: The path used by a LUN is always the one marked as preferred, unless that path is unavailable I use this policy is for Active/Active arrays. Fixed (fixed) uses only the active path.

3. Round Robin: Round robin (rr) uses the mru target selection policy and the any HBA selection policy to select paths.

4. Custom (custom) sets the LUN to expect a custom policy.

With Active- Passive storage array what multipathing policy you will choose?

I will use Fixed, or Preferred, path management policy to intelligently segment workload across both controllers.

Tell us a generic method to provision SAN Storage from any Array?

     I. Plan
    II. Validation with Support Matrix for Host Connectivity
   III. Provide Connectivity
   IV. Pick Volumes
    V. Make Meta Volumes if necessary
   VI. Map out Zoning
  VII. Map to storage arrays Ports
 VIII. Create Zones
   IX. LUN Mask
    X. Discover on Server

How will you discover SAN disks on Hosts?

Windows
Disk Management console, Diskmgmt.msc
HP-UX

Rescan the devices:
/usr/sbin/ioscan -C disk
    ioscan - scan the I/O system

SYNOPSIS
    driver | class] instance] hw_path] | [devfile]

    instance]

    driver | class] instance] hw_path] [devfile]

    driver | class] instance] lun hw_path] [devfile]

[devfile]

hw_path]

Generate device files: insf –e

Verify the new devices: ioscan funC

AIX

Rescan the devices: cfgmgr vl fcsx, x is FC adapter number

Verify the new devices: lsdev Cc

Linux

echo scsi add-single-device <host> <channel> <ID> <lun> > /proc/scsi/scsi

Solaris

Determine the FC channels: cfgadm -al

Force rescan: cfgadm o force_update c configure cx

Where x is the FC channel number

Force rescan at HBA port level: luxadm e forcelip /dev/fc/fpx

Force rescan on all FC devices: cfgadm al o show_FCP_dev

Install device files: devfsadm

Display all ports: luxadm e port

Display HBA port information luxadm -v display <WWPN>

Display HBA port information: luxadm e dump_map

To force Fibre Channel SAN disk rescan, Use device path from luxadm -e port output.

luxadm -e forcelip

ESX/ESXi
Sign in to VMware Infrastructure Client. Select the ESX host and then click the "Configuration" tab. Select "Storage Adapters" from under Hardware. Click "Rescan" ESXESXi 4.x and before

esxcfg-rescan
ESXi 5.x and later
esxcli storage core adapter rescan --all

How will you get the WWN of all your HBA's to provision SAN storage?

I. AIX

lscfg –v –l fcs#
(fcs – FC Adapter)
SMIT

II. HP-UX
fcmsutil /dev/td#
(td – Tachyon Adapter)
SAM

III. WIN:
emulexcfg –emc or

hbanywhere

I can use Storage Explorer to see detailed information about the Fibre Channel host bus adapters (HBAs).

IV. Solaris

/usr/sbin/lpfc/lputil

Also I can use:
more /var/adm/messages | grep –i wwn | more dmesg

V. VMware vSphere ESX/ESXi host

There are several ways to get HBA WWNs on VM

vSphere Client;
Using ESXi Shell;
Using Powershell / PowerCLI script.

VI. LINUX

/sys/class/scsi_host/hostN/device/fc_host/hostN/port_name

Where "N" is the number of device for your fibre HBAs

How will you find errors on various OS operating systems to troubleshoot problems?

I will check the OS log files/event logs for errors:

AIX: errpt -a
Windows: event logs
Solaris: /var/adm/messages
linux: /var/log/messages
HPUX: /var/adm/syslog/syslog.log
Tru64: /var/adm/syslog
SGI Irix: /var/adm/SYSLOG
ESX: /var/log/vmkernel
ESXi: /var/log/messages

For troubleshooting have you collected logs from a SAN Switch?

Yes.

I have been using Brocade Fabric and I have used "support save "to collect various logs for any issues.

 Syntax:

supportsave [os | platform | l2 | l3 | custom | core | all] <tftp server IP> <relative path> <user_tag>

What is Buffer-to-Buffer Credits?

Buffer credits, also called buffer-to-buffer credits (BBC) are used as a flow control method by Fibre Channel technology and represent the number of frames a port can store. Fibre Channel interfaces use buffer credits to ensure all packets are delivered to their destination. Flow-control mechanism to ensure that Fibre Channel switches do not run out of buffers, so that switches do not drop frames .overall performance can be boosted by optimizing the buffer-to-buffer credit allotted to each port.

How will you calculate Number of Buffers required?

Number of Buffers: BB_Credit = [port speed] x [round trip time] / [frame size]

Which load balancing policies are used between Inter Switch Links? Explain with an example?

I have used Brocade SAN and it has these load balancing policies:

I. DLS - Dynamic Load Sharing. FSPF link balancing by FSPF routing protocol

II. DPS - Dynamic Path Selection by effectively striping IOs at SCSI level

III. Frame-level load balancing - Each successive frame on a different physical ISL.

What best practices you will follow to setup ISL Trunking?

I. I will directly connect participating switches by Inter-Switch Link (ISL) cables.

II. I will keep the Trunk ports in the same port group

III. I will make sure Trunk ports run at the same speed

IV. I will ensure that all Trunk ports are set to the same ISL mode (L0 is the default).

V. I will convert Trunk ports to be E_Ports or EX_Ports

How will you decide how many storage arrays can be attached to a single host?

I will use:

Fan Out

For example 10:1.

I will determine this ratio, based on the server platform and performance requirement by consulting Storage vendors.

What is Drooping? How to check it?

Drooping= Bandwidth Inefficiency

Drooping begins if: BB_Credit<RTT/SF
Where RTT = Round Trip Time
SF = Serialization delay for a data frame

What Factors you will consider for designing a SAN?

I.   ISL over Subscription Ratio

II. SAN Fan–in and Fan-Out

III. Storage Ports

IV. Server I/O Profiles

V.   Fabric Features

VI. Continuity Requirements

Design should address three separate levels:

I.   Tier 1: 99.999% availability (5 minutes of downtime per year)
II. Tier 2: 99.9% availability (8.8 hours average downtime per year, 13.1 hours maximum)
III. Tier 3: 99% availability (3.7 days of downtime per year)

Explain your experience with disk sparing?

SAN Storage array has data integrity built into it.
A storage array uses spae disk drives to take the place of any disk drives that are blocked because of errors. Hot spares are available and will spare out predictively when a drive fails. There are tow types of disk sparing:

I. Dynamic Sparing: Data from the failed or blocked drive is copied directly to the new spare drive from the failing drive

II. Correction Copy: Data is regenerated from the remaining good drives in the parity group. For RAID 6, RAID 5, and RAID 1, after a failed disk has been replaced, the data is copied back to its original location, and the spare disk is then available.

Explain Brocade VCS Fabric technology?

Brocade VCS Fabric technology is used to build data center using automated networking architecture with Ethernet fabrics. Ethernet fabric is lossless, low latency, and convergence ready.

It works at Layer 2 by:

I. Distributed Fabric Services
II. Self-forming fabric
III. Master less Control
IV. Shared port profile information
V. Automatic Migration of Port Profiles
VI. Automatic distribution of zoning

Name a product for Ethernet Data Center Bridging (DCB)?

Brocade VDX 6720 family supports the emerging Ethernet Data Center Bridging (DCB), TRILL, and Fiber Channel over Ethernet (FCoE) standards,

What is the difference between multimode and single mode fibre?

Multimode fibre =large light carrying core, 62.5 microns or larger in diameter for short distance transmissions with LED based fibre optic equipment.
I have hand drawn a picture of Multimode Fibre core as you can see Multimode fibres have a much larger core than single-mode shown below (50, 62.5 μm or even higher), allowing light transmission through different paths

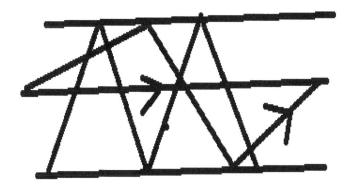

Single-mode fibre =small light carrying core of 8 to 10 microns in diameter used for long distance transmissions with laser diode based fibre optic transmission equipment.

A Single mode fibre core has a much smaller core, only about 9 microns, so that the light travels in only one ray as shown below.

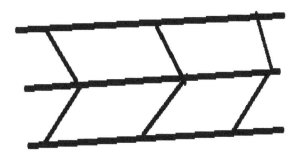

How to trouble shoot a fibre optic signal?

By using a Fibre Optic Loop back Fibre Optic Loop Back

Fig: Fibre Optic Loop Back

Fibre Optic Loop back modules are also called optical loopback adapters. I use the best practice of sending a loopback test to equipment, one at a time for isolating the problem

I have used different types:

LC loopback modules
SC loopback modules
MT-RJ fibre optic loop back
Others

It helps in testing the transmission capability and the receiver sensitivity of network equipment.

To use I connect One connector into the output port, while the other is plugged into the input port of the equipment.

Can you allocate a LUN larger than 2.19TB limit of MBR ?

I. I will use GPT.
II. GUID Partition Table, GPT is a part of the EFI standard that defines the layout of the partition table on a hard drive. GPT provides redundancy by writing the GPT header and partition table at the beginning of the disk and also at the end of the disk.

III. GPT Uses 64-bit LBA for storing Sector numbers. GPT disk can theoretically support up to 2^64 LBAs. Assuming 512 byte sector emulation, maximum capacity of a GPT disk = 9.4 x 10^21 bytes = 9.4 zettabytes (ZB)

Explain how BB Credits and port speeds are related?
Number of Buffers: BB_Credit = [port speed] x [round trip time] / [frame size]

How can you see the Load on the open systems connected to SAN?

Platform	Tool
AIX	iostat
HPUX	sar
	iostat
	Glance+
	vxstat
Linux	iostat
Windows	Performance Monitor
Solaris	iostat
Vmware	esxtop

How will you calculate IOPS per drive?

To calculate IOPS per drive the formula I will use is:
1000 / (Seek Time + Latency) = IOPS

How to calculate RPMs of SSD?

SSD drives have no movable parts and therefore have no RPM.

How will you calculate the required band width with write operations?

The required Bandwidth=the required bandwidth is determined by measuring the average number of write operations and the average size of write operations over a period of time.

How will you calculate Raw Capacity?

Raw Capacity= Usable + Parity

How do you know what type of fibre cable is needed?

I select it on the basis of transmission distance.
If the distance is less than a couple of miles, I will use multimode fibre cable.
If the distance is more than 3-5 miles, I will use single mode fibre cable.

Explain the Device Masking Architecture in storage arrays?

The device masking commands allow you to:

   I.   Assign and mask access privileges of hosts and adapters
   II. Connected in a Fibre Channel topology to storage arrays
and devices.

   III. Specify the host bus adapters (HBAs) through which a host can
access storage arrays devices.

   IV. Display or list device masking objects and their relationships:
Typical objects are hosts, HBAs, storage arrays devices, and Fibre
Channel Adapter (FA) ports.

   V.   Modify properties, such as names and access privileges associated with device
       masking objects (for example, change the Name of a host).

Explain SAN zoning?

SAN zoning is a method of arranging Fibre Channel devices into logical groups over the
physical configuration of the fabric.

SAN zoning may be utilized to implement compartmentalization of data for security
purposes.

Each device in a SAN may be placed into multiple zones.

The base components of zoning are
   I.   Zones
   II. Zone sets

III. Default zone
IV. Zone members

A zone is a set of devices that can access each other through port-to-port connections. When you create a zone with a certain number of devices, only those devices are permitted to communicate with each other. This means that a device that is not a member of the zone cannot access devices that belong to the zone.

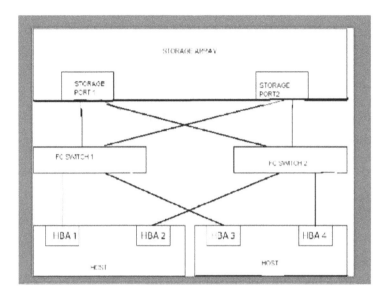

Figure shows the SAN Connectivity and accordingly zoning must be done.

What is the difference between Hard and Soft Zoning?

Hard zoning is zoning which is implemented in hardware.

Soft zoning is zoning which is implemented in software.

Hard zoning physically blocks access to a zone from any device outside of the zone.

Soft zoning uses filtering implemented in fibre channel switches to prevent ports from being seen from outside of their assigned zones. The security vulnerability in soft zoning is that the ports are still accessible if the user in another zone correctly guesses the fibre channel address.

What is Port Zoning?

Port zoning utilizes physical ports to define security zones. A user's access to data is determined by what physical port he or she is connected to. With port zoning, zone information must be updated every time a user changes switch ports. In addition, port zoning does not allow zones to overlap. Port zoning is normally implemented using hard zoning, but could also be implemented using soft zoning.

What is WWN zoning?

WWN zoning uses name servers in the switches to either allow or block access to particular World Wide Names (WWNs) in the fabric. A major advantage of WWN zoning is the ability to recable the fabric without having to redo the zone information. WWN zoning is susceptible to unauthorized access, as the zone can be bypassed if an attacker is able to spoof the World Wide Name of an authorized HBA.

What is LUN, Logical Unit Number?

A Logical Unit Number or LUN is a logical reference to entire physical disk, or a subset of a larger physical disk or disk volume or portion of a storage subsystem.

What is LUN masking?

LUN (Logical Unit Number) Masking is an authorization process that makes a LUN available to some hosts and unavailable to other hosts.
LUN Masking is implemented primarily at the HBA (Host Bus Adapter) level. LUN Masking implemented at this level is vulnerable to any attack that compromises the HBA. Some storage controllers also support LUN Masking.

Why we need LUN Masking?

LUN Masking is important because Windows based servers attempt to write volume labels to all available LUN's. This can render the LUN's unusable by other operating systems and can result in data loss.
Device masking lets you control your host HBA access to certain storage arrays devices. A device masking database, based in the storage arrays unit, eliminates conflicts through centralized monitoring and access records. Both HBA and storage arrays director ports in their Channel topology are uniquely identified by a 64-bit World Wide Name (WWN). For ease of use, you can associate an ASCII World Wide Name (AWWN) with each WWN.

How all switches and directors in the fabric maintain the same zoning information?

I. Zoning in a Fiber Channel fabric is managed on a fabric-wide basis.
II. Registered State Change Notification (RSCN) messages are sent to inform attached devices when zoning changes occur.

Explain NPIV?

I. N_Port ID Virtualization (NPIV) is an ANSI T11 standard.

II. With NPIV a single Fibre Channel HBA port (single N_Port/single FCID) can register with several World Wide Port Names (WWPNs) or multiple N_Port IDs in the SAN fabric.

III. NPIV allows a fabric-attached N_Port to claim multiple fabric addresses.
IV. Each address appears as a unique entity on the Fibre Channel fabric.

Why you will use N-Port Virtualization?

I. N_Port ID Virtualization, NPIV Allows multiple Logical Partitions to share a single FCP channel => Uses fewer FCP channels
II. Better channel utilization and simpler infrastructure
III. In a virtual machine environment each VM will have separate WWPNs

How will you ensure that SAN-attached tape devices are represented consistently in a host operating system?

I will use the Persistent Binding for Tape Devices.

Persistent binding is a host-centric enforced way of directing an operating system to assign certain SCSI target IDs and LUNs.

Persistent Name Binding support is for target devices.

Persistent binding is provided for users to associate a specified device World Wide Port Name (WWPN) to a specified SCSI target ID.

For example, where a specific host will always assign SCSI ID 3 to the first router it finds, and LUNs 0, 1, and 2 to the three-tape drives attached to the router.

Practical examples:

For Emulex HBA on a Solaris host for setting up persistent binding:
 # lputil
MAIN MENU

1. List Adapters
2. Adapter Information
3. Firmware Maintenance
4. Reset Adapter
5. Persistent Bindings

Using option 5 will perform a manual persistent binding and the file is: /kernel/drv/lpfc.conf file.

lpfc.conf file looks like:

fcp-bind-WWNN="50060XY484411 c6c11:lpfc0t1",
"50060XY4411 c6c12:lpfc1t2";

sd.conf file looks like:

name="sd" parent="lpfc" target=1 lun=0;

name="sd" parent="lpfc" target=2 lun=0;
Reconfigure:

touch /reconfigure
shutdown -y -g0 -i6

Have you used CLI to create Zones on a SAN switch?

Yes, on brocade:

I. I will create an alias.

aliCreate "aliname", "member; member"

II. I will create a zone.

zonecreate "Zone Name", "alias1; alias2"

III. I will add the zone to the defined configuration.

cfgadd "ConfigName", "ZoneXYZ"

cfgadd "configuration_Name", "Zone_name"

IV. I will   save the defined configuration to persistent storage.

cfgsave

V. I will   enable the configuration.

cfgenable "ConfigName"

cfgenable " configuration_Name "

Explain your experience of SAN switch firmware update via CLI?

I have updated Brocade firmware via CLI:

I. configupload: Saves the switch config as an ASCII text file to an FTP server
II. configdownload: To restore a switch configuration from ASCII text file

Explain your experience in managing SAN switch ports via CLI?

I have administered Brocade ports via CLI:

A. portcfgshow Displays the port settings
B. portname To assign a name for a port

C. portdisable To disable a port or slot
D. portenable To enable a port or slot

What are the types of IOPS?

    I. Total IOPS
    II. Random Read IOPS
    III. Random Write IOPS
    IV. Sequential Read IOPS
    V. Sequential Write IOPS

What is the Small block random I/O for various disk types?

$$IOPS = \frac{1}{(\text{average latency}) + (\text{average seek time})}$$

Accordingly:

    I. Fibre Channel 15k RPM: 180 IOPS
    II. SAS 15k RPM: 180 IOPS
    III. Enterprise flash drives (EFDs): 2500 IOPS

Explain your experience with Offloaded Data Transfer (ODX)?

    I. I can use the Offloaded Data Transfers (ODX) feature of Windows Server 2012 to copy files from one LUN to another LUN.

    II. With Offloaded Data Transfer (ODX) Windows Server 2012 on SAN the move or copy actions directly via SAN, bypassing the host, which removes any performance hit on the Windows Server host and allows the SAN to perform the actions much faster.

III. With ODX, the actual copying of the data is handled by the storage system and will not add any additional traffic to the primary network.

IV. When a server is connected to a storage array such as a SAN, it has access to very powerful hardware designed to move and copy data.

How will you backup large amount of data on heterogeneous network attached storage? How to set it up?

I will use Network Data Management Protocol (NDMP) to perform backups over Fibre Channel.

With NDMP data can bypass backup servers; it increases the speed and efficiency of NAS data protection.

Backup data flows from the storage system to the NAS filer to an attached tape library unit (TLU) without traversing the network.

Here are the steps:

I. Set up NAS/ File server
II. Run Fibre Cables
III. Zone tape drive(s) to be seen by the NDMP host
IV. Verify the NDMP host/ can see and access the tape drive(s)
V. Create the ndmp login name and password
   If it's Netbackup:

   NetBackup can carry out any backup operation once I authorize NDMP host the access, I will execute the following command on master/media server:
   <install_path>/volmgr/bin/set_ndmp_attr -auth<ndmp-host>< username> (Solaris)
   set_ndmp_attr -auth filer_hostname password
   set_ndmp_attr -verify

What is a Multimode Fibre Cable?

Multimode fibre cable has large light carrying core and is usually used for short distance data transmission.

Suitable for distances of up to about 10 miles

Typical multimode fibre optic cables are 62.5/125 and 50/125 types

Fig: Multimode Fibre Cable

Explain your experience with data encryption in SAN environment?

I. Host Encryption: I have used CLARiiON Host Encryption to protect information in EMC CLARiiON storage environments to comply with Payment Card Industry Data Security Standard PCI DSS. It uses a centralized enterprise key management and lets me choose the LUNs or volumes that contain sensitive data.

II. Data at rest encryption: This Encryption provides hardware-based, on-array, back-end encryption. Data at Rest Encryption provides encryption on the back end in Fibre Channel I/O modules that incorporate XTS-AES 256-bit data-at-rest encryption.

> VSP data at rest encryption: It's built into Hitachi Virtual Storage Platform (VSP) and Hitachi Universal Storage Platform® V and VM via encrypting backend directors (EBED)
>
> EMC Symmetrix data at rest encryption: This is a data at rest encryption on the back end using Fibre Channel I/O modules that incorporate XTS-AES 256-bit data-at-rest encryption and RSA Embedded Key Manager for key management.

III. Disk encryption: I have used data encryption built into the Hitachi Adaptable Modular Storage 2000 family via self-encrypting drives.

IV. Fabric OS encryption:

Brocade has an encryption solution that resides in a Storage Area Network (SAN) fabric that works transparently with heterogeneous servers, disk Storage subsystems, and tape libraries. Data entering the SAN from a server is encrypted before it is written to storage. This is accomplished via an engine, Cleartext is sent from the server to the encryption engine, where it is encrypted into ciphertext using one of two encryption.

Where you encrypt Data Stored in SAN?

For stored data encryption I can enable encryption in SAN array.
Encryption can be done at drive, LUN or volume level.
Data is encrypted / decrypted by the array or device upon ingress / egress.

Explain your experience with Data Deduplication?

Deduplication = Duplicate data is deleted. It reduces the required storage capacity since only the unique data is stored.

Two types of data deduplication are:

I. Post-process and
II. Inline deduplication

Post-process deduplication starts after the data has been written to the storage volume in a separate process. There will not be degradation in performance.

During inline deduplication, deduplication is handled in real time as the data is written to the storage volume less storage is required, because. There will be degradation in performance.

For example Avamar deduplicates backup data at the client before transfer across the LAN or WAN during a backup operation.

ProtecTIER® Deduplication Appliance Express leverages unique data deduplication technology can be configured with either a Virtual Tape Library (VTL) or Symantec OpenStorage (OST) interface.

Have you used short stroking?

Short stroking is the technique of storing less data on a hard disk drive than its maximum capacity and concentrating that data on the outer diameter. As a result, these outer sectors can be read faster (MB/s) than those near the center of the platter. Short stroking reduces latency and increases performances by reducing seek times.

Explain N Port virtualization? Which switch supports NPV?

N Port virtualization (NPV): NPV allows an Edge Switch to Behave as an HBA to the Core Switch. It reduces the number of Fibre Channel domain IDs in SANs.
NPV is supported by the Cisco MDS 9000.

How to use SAN over long distance?

I will use Long-Distance Trunking over dark fibre, CWDM, DWDM, or SONET.

Explain various connectivity options for long distance replication?

I had seen exponential increase in user demand for bandwidth so I choose from:

	Dark Fibre	CWDM	DWDM	SONET/SDH	IP
Distance in KM	40	100	200	1000	Unlimited
Latency in us/km	5	5	Low	Medium	Variable
Bandwidth in Gbps	100	8 Channels, 2.5Gbps	100 Channels 40Gbps	OC-192 10Gbps	Variable
Cost	Low	Low	High	Medium	High

WDM (Wavelength Division Multiplexing): It uses of optical fibres to achieve higher speeds. It uses wavelengths to multiplex users. It allows for continuous channel allocation per user and hence Increases the effective bandwidth of existing fibre.

DWDM (Dense Wave Digital Multiplexing): Dense wavelength division multiplexing (DWDM) is a fibre-optic transmission technique that employs light wavelengths to transmit data parallel-by-bit or serial-by-character. Up to 80 wavelengths of data can be multiplexed into a light stream transmitted on a single optical fibre.

For example:

Cisco DWDM systems provides high density, 32-channel (lambda) aggregation between data centers up to 320 km apart.
Each channel can operate up to 10 Gbps for a total of 320 Gbps over a single fibre pair.

What factors affect IOPS?

3 Key Factors:

1. Rotational speed revolutions per minute (RPM)
2. Average latency. The time taken by the sector of the disk being accessed to rotate into position under a read/write head.
3. Averages seek time. The time (in ms) it takes for the hard drive's read/write head to position itself over the track being read or written.

How will you calculate the maximum number of concurrent I/O requests on AIX?

The number of concurrent I/O requests is important to calculate the number of data paths:

32-bit kernel:

(4 + number of LUs) x 64 + 2560

64-bit kernel:

(4 + number of LUs) x 128 + 2560

How can I use exit status in UNIX to see if a command ran successfully?

$ echo $?
0
If I get exit status as zero, the command executed successfully.

Which Commands you can use in UNIX for Data Migration?

Cpio

To Copy files from one directory tree to another use cpio

To copy the files of the present directory, and sub-directories to a new directory called newdir:

> find . -depth -print0 | cpio --null -pvd newdir

cd /source/directory/

find . -depth -print | cpio -pduvm /destination/directory

<u>tar</u>

tar command is useful for storing a number of files in one file ,traditionally on a magnetic tape, but it can be done on another file.

To copy :

>cd /<source directory>

>tar -cf - * | (cd /<target directory>;tar -xf -)

Also Creating a new directory called destdir for the files to be copied into

$ tar cpf - . | (mkdir /tmp/destdir ; cd /tmp/destdir; tar xvpf -)

What type of connectors are 10G SFP modules?

LC-type GBIC

Explain the types of fibre optic cable connectors?

ST Connectors: Slotted bayonet type connector with long ferrule, it's a Common connector for multimode fibres

Fig: ST Connectors

FC Connectors: Screw on type connector.
Single mode fibres

fig.: FC Connectors

SC Connectors: Push/pull connector that can also be used with duplex fibre construction.

Fig: SC Connectors

LC Connectors: Much like the ST connector but with a ferrule that is half the size.

Fig: LC Connectors

MT-RJ Connectors: Connector configured for duplex fibres with both fibres in one ferrule.

MU Connectors: Much like the SC connector, ferrule about half the size.

What are the different types of fibre optic cable based on fibre types?

Three types:

  I. Single Mode Fibre Optic Cable
 II. Multimode Fibre Optic Cable
III. Hybrid/Composite Cable

Explain specifications of Mode Conditioning Fiber Optic Cables?

Supported distances of the various 50-micron cables:

	Data rate/Link speed	M5 (OM2) cable	M5E (OM3) cable	M5F (OM4) cable
1	8 Gbps	50 m (164 ft.)	150 m (492 ft.)	190 m (623 ft.)
2	4 Gbps	150 m (492 ft.)	380 m (1 247 ft.)	400 m (1312 ft.)
3	2 Gbps	300 m (984 ft.)	Not specified	Not specified
4	1 Gbps	500 m (1640 ft.)	Not specified	Not specified

Supported distances of the various 62.5-micron cables:

Speed	Length
1.0625 Gb	2 m (6.6 ft) min to 300 m (985 ft) max
2.125 Gb	2 m (6.6 ft) min to 150 m (492 ft) max
4 Gb	2 m (6.6 ft) min to 70 m (231 ft) max

In Storage area networks speed of various components currently you have?

4-Gbps Fibre Channel switches, host bus adapters (HBAs) and hard drives.

Where have you used GBIC? What you do if GBIC fails?

I have used GBIC in SAN switches to transmit data over a SAN.

I always use WWN zoning so if there is a GBIC failure, I switch the FC cable to a different GBIC without the need of rezoning.

What is SFP?

Transmits and receives data while connected to switches and routers and allows them to communicate over a SAN.

Fig: SFP

What is SAS?

Serial Attached SCSI (SAS)

Serial Attached SCSI uses serial signaling technology.
It is a point-to-point serial protocol that replaces the parallel SCSI. It provides multi-initiator support and full duplex communication.
 It has Full-duplex with link aggregation, 6.0 Gbit/s. SAS enables multiple devices (up to 128) of different sizes and types to be connected simultaneously.

Fig: SAS Connector

Dust particles and contamination cause signal loss across fiber optic connectors, which guidelines you will follow for connector inspection and cleaning?

I will follow TIA TSB-140 Additional Guidelines for Field Testing Length, Loss and Polarity of Optical Fiber Cabling Systems.

The TIA/TSB 140 standard requires testing each fiber link with an Optical Loss Test Set (OLTS) kit for Attenuation.

It has these two Types of testing's:

Tier 1: testing of attenuation with an optical loss test set (OLTS) and verifying the cabling length and polarity.
Tier 1 testing – with Light Source and Power Meter (LSMP) or Optical Loss Test Set (OLTS).
Maximum allowable attenuation is as follows:

Strand type	Wavelength (nm)	Maximum attenuation (dB)
A. Multi-mode	850	1.82 dB
B. Single-	1310 or 1550	1.59 dB

mode		

Tier 2: by using optical time domain reflectometer (OTDR) trace.

For testing I will use MultiFiber Pro.
Fluke Networks MultiFiber Pro Optical Power Meter and Fiber Test Kits

The MultiFiber Pro from fluke meter includes:

A single "Scan All" test function that automatically tests all 12 fibers in an MPO connector.
Built-in polarity verification for end-to-end connectivity of MPO trunk cables.
Innovative, intuitive user interface to display all 12 fiber test results.

For cleaning I will use Fluke Networks Fiber Optic Cleaning Kits:
The complete solution for precision end-face fiber optic cable cleaning.
Contains everything needed to eliminate the main cause of fiber link failure: contamination.
It has solvent pen which precisely dispenses specially formulated fiber cleaning solution.

Have you used Disk Write Patrol in SAN?

In a SAN Storage Array a Disk Patrol read checks for physical disk errors that could lead to drive failure. Patrol reading checks for bad blocks on each storage device in an array. These checks usually include an attempt at corrective action.
For example ETERNUS disk storage systems data are protected via a disk drive patrol function. An internal controller regularly checks the disk drives, in background, to detect errors and write failures.

I have used three types of disk patrol functions in Fujitsu Storage:
   I. Read Patrol,
  II. Write Patrol, and
 III. Data compare check.

I have seen that a Disk Write Patrol causes repeated accesses to the same area on the disk drive. Disk Write Patrol causes an increase of disk failures due to write errors in the disk patrol area. This repeated access pattern is known to be causing an increase in read/write errors in the diagnostic area. The ratio of errors may increase sufficiently to cause the disk to be proactively failed. So I will disable the Disk Write Patrol function.

Explain Thick Provision Lazy Zeroed Virtual disk?

In this virtual volume the write of the user data is delayed until the initial zeroing operation which is done directly to the disk bypassing the cache.

The block zero processing for "Lazy Zeroed thick" virtual machines is delayed until a write to the location is issued. Just before user data is written to a block for the first time, the block is zeroed. That's why the size of the VMDK on the data store is same as the size of the virtual disk that was created.

Which types of virtual disks you have used?

There are three formats of virtual disks for VM's:

I. Thin: size of the VMDK is as much as the amount of data written out from the VM.
II. Lazy Zero Thick: The size of the VMDK on the data store is same as the size of the virtual disk that was created.
III. Eager Zero Thick: With Eager Zero Thick, the VMDK is pre-zeroed and assigned to the guest during provisioning of the VMFS volume. An eager zeroed thick disk has all space allocated and wiped clean of any previous contents on the physical media at creation time. It's good for any high IO Virtual Machine.
IV. Thick: A thick disk has all space allocated at creation time.
V. Thin: Space is allocated but zeroed on demand as the space is used.

What are the various types of LUN Volumes?

I. Masked - The volume is exposed to the storage port and to the host.

II. Unmasked - The volume is exposed to the storage port, but not to the host.

III. Unmapped – The volume is not exposed to the storage port..

IV. Free Extents – Available free extents that can be used to create a meta volume.

How will you Transfer a file using network?

I will use File Transfer Protocol (FTP) , a standard network protocol to transfer files from one file to another over a TCP-based network

Use ftp Command

Example a: To connect to the machine bottoml.net, then change directory to bottomlined, then download the file bottomlinetest:

```
> ftp bottoml.net,

 ftp> cd bottomlined
   250 CWD command successful.
 ftp> get bottomlinetest
 ftp> quit
```

to upload the file blt

```
 ftp> put blt
 ftp> quit
```

The ftp program by default sends files in ascii (text) format unless changed to binary mode:

```
 ftp> binary
 ftp> put foo
```

The file foo transferred in binary mode

```
 ftp> ascii
 ftp> get foo1
```

The File Foo1 Transferred In Ascii Mode

How will you Remove Cores on UNIX?

To find and remove core files interactively:

> find ~ -name core -exec file {} \; -exec rm -i {} \;

Explain iSCSI naming conventions?

iSCSI has two schemes for naming nodes (initiators or targets
iqn (iSCSI qualified name) — Based on reverse Domain Name System (DNS)
eui (extended unique identifier) — same as FC World-Wide Names.

IQN - iSCSI Qualfied Name Format:

This iSCSI name type can be used by any organization which owns a domain name. This naming format is useful when an end user or service provider wishes to assign iSCSI names for targets and/or initiators.

```
              Org.       Subgroup Naming Authority
              Naming
Type  Date    Auth
+-++------+ +--------+ +------------------------------+
```

iSCSI Qualified Name (IQN) Format
The IQN format takes the form iqn.yyyy-mm.naming-authority:unique name, where:
yyyy-mm is the year and month when the naming authority was established.
naming-authority is usually reverse syntax of the Internet domain name of the naming authority.
¦unique name is any name you want to use, for example, the name of your host.

Explain EUI - Extended Unique Identifier Format?

The IEEE defined 64-bit extended unique identifier (EUI-64) is a concatenation of a 24-bit Organizationally Unique Identifier (OUI) value administered by the IEEE Registration Authority and a 40-bit extension identifier assigned by the organization with that OUI assignment.
```
N
 A  OUI    VSID
 A
|-|-------|-----------|
```

The EUI format takes the form eui.16 hex digits.

What are some of the best practices for SAN Designing?

I. Use Single Initiator zoning with separate zones for tape and disk traffic. Zoning should be with single HBA zoning (One HBA & One Storage port per zone)

II. LUN Masking – Each LUN should be mapped to mirrored Storage ports

III. Masking configured to allow a host WWN to see the specific LUN on its designated Storage port.

IV. Dynamic multi-pathing should be used for load balancing.

What is the fan-out ratio?

The fan out ratio is the qualified maximum number of initiators per storage port.
Eg: if Server A, B, C is accessing Storage port-A. The fan out ratio would be 3:1

What is the expansion fan-in ratio?

Its qualified maximum number of storage connections to a particular server or maximum number of storage ports that can be accessed by a single initiator through a SAN. Eg: Server A can access storage from Storage A, B, C, So the fan in ratio is 1:3

How will you calculate ISL oversubscription?

ISL Oversubscription= the Ratio of Device Ports to Exports= Number of Hosts /Number of ISL's.

On UNIX systems how will you remove a hung process?

Kill

Kill Command

Purpose

Sends a signal to running processes.

Syntax

To Send Signal to Processes

kill [-s { SignalName | SignalNumber }] ProcessID ...

Programs can choose to ignore certain signals by trapping signals with a special handler.

One signal they cannot ignore is signal 9. It's a sure way of killing

kill -9 126

Signal 1, or `HUP' can be sent to certain programs by the superuser.

kill -1   <inetd>
kill -HUP <inetd>

which forces `inetd' to reread its configuration file.

kill -20 <PID>   # suspend process <PID>
kill -18 <PID>   # resume process <PID>

Explain the I/O Data Path in a SAN?

    I. Path of the data I/O
   II. Starts at the application
  III. Goes to the storage system
  IV. Returns back to the application

I trace the I/O data path from application to spindle, I/O Journey starts and ends at the application as:

Application <> HOST/HBA <> SAN Switch/Director <> Storage Array

Also I will take in-depth look at the I/O data Inside the Storage Array:

Storage Array <> Array Port <>CHP<>Cache<>ACP<>Disk (Hard disk drive consists of a spindle on which the platters spin at a constant RPM while the read-write heads locate and exchange data)

How will you know which software and HBAs are supported by a Storage array?

Support Matrix

Explain the role of Fibre channel layers?

Fibre channel Layer	Roles
FC - 4	Defines how a Fibre Channel network will communicate with upper level applications (Audio / Video / IPI / SCSI / HIPPI / IP / 802.2)
FC - 3	For advanced features: Striping, Hunt groups, Multicast
FC - 2	Similar to the MAC (Media Access Layer) and defines how data from upper level applications is split into frames for transport over the lower layers (Framing Protocol / Flow Control)
FC - 1	Defines how frames are encoded and decoded for transport (Encode / Decode). The information transmitted over a fibre is encoded 8 bits at a time into a 10 bit Transmission Character.
FC - 0	Defines the various media types that can carry Fibre Channel data (Single, Multimode, Copper: 133Mb, 266Mb, 531Mb, 1.06G, 2.12G & 4.25G)

When you will use VLAN Tagging?

I. VLAN Tagging is used when a link needs to carry traffic for more than one VLAN. It allows controlling network traffic.
II. A unique packet identifier is added within each header.
III. Upon reaching the destination node (Switch) the VLAN ID is removed from the packet by the adjacent switch and forwarded to the attached device.
IV. Its a mechanism for controlling the flow of broadcasts and applications
V. Types: Cisco proprietary Inter-Switch Link (ISL) and IEEE 802.1Q.

Which HBA you recommend? Why?

I know that QLogic 4Gb HBAs deliver the industries highest performance.

QLogic's HBAs are the number one choice of users for all generations of FC technologies because:

QLogic HBAs have 246% higher Sequential Write Performance
than Emulex . Higher by 95,000 IOPs.
QLogic HBAs have 79% higher Sequential Read Performance than
Emulex . Higher by 67,000 IO. On Oracle workloads, QLogic's dual port HBAs delivered 28% more IOPs than Emulex.

What flag you will set when sharing director ports between hosts with multiple vendor operating systems? How?

SPC-2 is a SCSI reserve and release method.

SPC-2 flag can be set up by port or by initiator.

In environments sharing director ports between hosts with multiple vendor operating systems, I will ensure that all host operating systems are capable of supporting the SPC-2 functionality before enabling it on the port.

If any OS sharing the affected director port does not support SPC-2 functionality, the SPC-2 bit cannot be set on a per-port basis and must be set on a per-initiator basis per-initiator basis by using Solutions Enabler CLI if it EMC SAN and by Hitachi Unified Storage Command Line Interface if it HITACHI SAN.

aughopt-unit uni_name -set ctl_no port_no

-gno group_no | -gname group_name

-platform NotSpecified | HP | Solaris | AIX | Linux |

Windows | VMware | NetWare

-middleware NotSpecified | VCS | TruCluster

Description

This command references or sets the host group options

When specifying per option (For 9500V, AMS and WMS)

-SPC2 ctl_no port_no group_no enable | disable

Specify whether to set the SPC-2 Mode effective or ineffective.

ctl_no : Controller number (0, 1).

port_no : Port number (A, B, C, D).

group_no: Host Group number.

enable : Enables the SPC-2 Mode.

disable : Disables the SPC-2 Mode.

Explain TCQ?

Tagged Command Queuing (TCQ) allows the operating system to send multiple read and write requests to a hard drive. I have used it in SAS drives. It copies better under heavy loads.

Explain CRC?

CRC: Cyclic Redundancy Check is a self-test for error detection and correction.

It's a parity bit based error detection scheme.

The CRC is based on:

    I. Polynomial division

    II. Arithmetic over the field of integers mod 2

As a SAN administrator you need to schedule a job on UNIX? What command you can use?

I will Cron.

Cron

cron is a unix, solaris utility that allows tasks to be automatically run in the background at regular intervals by the cron daemon..

Crontab Commands

export EDITOR=vi ;to specify a editor to open crontab file.

crontab -e   Edit your crontab file, or create one if it doesn't already exist.
crontab -l   Display your crontab file.
crontab -r   Remove your crontab file.
crontab -v   Display the last time you edited your crontab file. (This option is only available on a few systems.)

Crontab file

A crontab file has five fields for specifying day , date and time followed by the command to be run at that interval.


```
*   *  *  *   *  command to be executed

-   -  -  -  -

|  |  |  |  |

|  |  |  |  +----- day of week (0 - 6) (Sunday=0)

|  |  |  +------- month (1 - 12)

|  |  +--------- day of month (1 - 31)

|  +----------- hour (0 - 23)

+------------- min (0 - 59)
```

Crontab Example


```
#minute (0-59),
#|    hour (0-23),
#|    |    day of the month (1-31),
#|    |    |    month of the year (1-12),
#|    |    |    |    day of the week (0-6 with 0=Sunday).
#|    |    |    |    |    commands
```

0   2   *   *   0,4   /etc/cron.d/logchecker

Explain Credit?

I. A numeric value that represents the maximum number of receive buffers provided by an F/FL_Port to its attached N/NL_Port such that the N/NL_Port may transmit frames without overrunning the F/FL_Port.

II. Buffer-to-buffer credits (BB_credits) are a flow-control mechanism to ensure that Fibre Channel switches do not run out of buffers, so that switches do not drop frames.

III. BB_credits are negotiated on a per-hop basis.

IV. The receive BB_credit (fcrxbbcredit) value may be configured for each Fibre Channel interface.

V. The receive BB_credit values depend on the module type and the port mode.

What are the components of HBA drivers?

There are two components:

I. The port drivers
II. The miniport drivers

The port driver is the portion of the driver that adds the support for the hardware device itself to the Operating system. For example FC functions. This adds support to the OS for FC functionality in general and houses basic operations at the FC level.

The Miniport driver is provided by the hardware manufacturer of the HBA. This portion of the driver adds additional support for their specific HBA's.
For example persistent binding functionality.

Have you replaced a HBA?

I. I will   stop all I/O to the storage systems connected to the HBA I am replacing.

II. I will shut down the operating system on the server with the HBA I am replacing.

III. I will disconnect any storage groups/LUNs connected to the server through the HBA.

IV. I will remove the HBA from the server.

V. I will set the HBA jumpers on the new HBA to enable it for use with the host.

VI. I will install the adapter card and cables.

VII. I will connect the power and allow the system to boot normally.

VIII. I upgrade to make sure driver versions and the firmware versions are up-to-date.

IX. I will set HBA configuration to Fabric

X. I will ensure that the new HBA has performed a Fabric Login to the switch.

XI. Now I will modify the zoning configuration to remove the old defective HBA and add the new HBA.

XII. Now I will reconnect any Storage Groups and or LUNs disconnected earlier.

Which specifications you check for HDD reliability?

I. MTTF = Mean Time To Failure
II. MTTR = Mean Time To Repair
III. MTBF = Mean Time Between Failures = MTTF + MTTR
IV. MTBF = (Total Time of all Parts run) / (Total number of failures)

Why you use switched fabric?

Because it provides Maximum possible number of node ports in a switched fabric.
For example:
Domain ID is a unique number provided to each switch in the fabric and since
239 addresses are available for a domain ID:
Maximum possible number of node ports in a switched fabric:
239 domains x 256 areas x 256 ports = 15,663,104

On a Microsoft Windows Server you are unable to initialize master boot record (MBR) disks and you get error message "the disk is write protected ". What can you do?

I will use the "diskpart clean all" command in Windows to zero every sector on a disk.
DiskPart is a text-mode command interpreter in Windows OS.
This tool allows managing objects (disks, partitions, or volumes).

Steps to clean a disk:

This command will clean only the first 1MB of data on the disk which would include the MBR:

  I. DISKPART> select disk X

 II. DISKPART> clean

     This command will zero out every sector on the entire disk:

III. DISKPART> select disk X

IV. DISKPART> clean all

Here are various options:

LIST DISK
List all the available disks on the system.
SELECT DISK N
Choose a disk by number.
CLEAN
Erase a disk entirely. Partition table and all partitions are erased. This command can only be executed after issuing a SELECT DISK command.
CONVERT TYPE
Create the partition table for the disk. This command can only be executed after issuing a SELECT DISK command. Type can be BASIC or DYNAMIC for converting between the types of disk; type can be MBR or GPT for converting between types of partition table. GPT has a minimum size restriction.
CREATE PARTITION TYPE SIZE=N
Creates a partition of the given type of size N.
LIST PARTITION

List all the available partitions on the current disk. This command can only be executed after issuing a SELECT DISK command.
SELECT PARTITION N
Select a partition by number. This command can only be executed after issuing a SELECT DISK command.
FORMAT FS=TYPE LABEL=TEXT
Format the current partition. This command can only be executed after issuing a SELECT PARTITION command. Type is either FAT or NTFS. LABEL is a string that appears in Windows Explorer that helps identify the partition. If the string has spaces, enclose the string in quotes.
LIST VOLUME
List information on all the volumes on all disks.

You need to reclaim free space while migrating from a Thick to a Thin Volume. Can you use UNIX utilities such as migratepv?

I have noticed that migrating to thin devices using migratepv does not reclaim expected amount of free space.

We need to see what this command does:

migratepv Command
Purpose
Moves allocated physical partitions from one physical volume to one or more other physical volumes.
Syntax
migratepv [-i] [-l LogicalVolume] SourcePhysicalVolume DestinationPhysicalVolume..
Description
The migratepv command moves allocated physical partitions and the data they contain from the SourcePhysicalVolume to one or more other physical volumes.

It performs its migration based on the type of data on the source device.

Using migratepv does not recover free space, as it will copy every logical extent from the source volume to the target volume regardless of the contents.

To reclaim free space I will use cpio or cp to copy the data from the thick devices to the thin devices.

Explain your experience with SAN Topologies

I have used three types of topologies:

I. PTP (point to point): I have used it for DAS configurations.

II. FC-AL (FC Arbitrated Loop): Fabric Loop ports, or FL ports on a switch, and NL_Ports (node loop) on an HBA, I have used it to support loop operations.

III. FC-SW (FC Switched): I have used this mode when operating on a switched SAN. Fibre Channel Switched Fabric (FC-SW): A fibre channel configuration in which the devices are connected in a network using a fibre channel switch. The full bandwidth of the fibre channel is available to all the devices. Fibre Channel topology that consists of up to 16,777,216(224) devices, each of which is connected to a Fibre Channel switch.

Name the main types of storage network components?

Storage network components are devices that help store and transmit data over a network.

I. Node
II. Ports
III. World Wide Name (WWN)
IV. Host bus adapter (HBA)
V. Cables
VI. Protocols

Which Cloud service is related with Storage?

Cloud infrastructure as a service (IaaS)

Explain the concept of Frames in SAN?

I. Frames are the basic building blocks of an FC connection.

II. The Frames contain the information to be transmitted called Payload and address of the source and destination ports and link control information.

III. Frames are broadly categorized as Data frames and Link control frames.

IV. Data frames may be used as Link_Data frames and Device_Data frames, link control frames are classified as Acknowledge (ACK) and Link_Response (Busy and Reject) frames.

V. The primary function of the Fabric is, to receive the Frames from the source port and route them to the destination port.

VI. It is the FC-2 layer's responsibility to break the data to be transmitted into Frame size, and reassemble the Frames.

How will you find HBA's on AIX?

lsconfig -vl fcs0

How will you find HBA's on ESxi?

/proc/scsi/qlaxxx/

How will you check the RAID table for corruption in LINUX?

Using /proc/mdstat.

mdadm - manage MD devices aka Linux Software RAID
Synopsis
mdadm [mode] <raiddevice> [options] <component-devices>
Description
RAID devices are virtual devices created from two or more real block devices. This allows multiple devices (typically disk drives or partitions thereof) to be combined into a single device to hold (for example) a single file system. Some RAID levels include redundancy and so can survive some degree of device failure.

Have you used Traffic Isolation Zoning?

Yes.

    I.   I have used it to dedicate an ISL to high priority host to target traffic.

    II. To control the flow of inter switch traffic by creating a dedicated path for a set of N-Ports.

How you make your SAN ready for heterogeneous switches?

I will put   SAN Fabric Switches in interoperability (or interop) mode.

Here are the interop modes for brocade:

Interop 0, native; 1, open fabric; 2, McData; 3, open fabric;

Can you migrate to a new SAN Switch without downtime?

Yes.

    I.   I will check that all hosts are connected to at least two fabrics
    II. I will ensure that all paths are working correctly
    III. Replace the Switch
    IV. Then I will change the switch Domain ID
    V. Then I will configure all new paths on all hosts connected to the new switch

Give a generic high level method to setup ISCSI

    I.   I will enable Target Security
    II. Then I will create additional targets
    III. I will edit the targets
    IV. I will Map LUNs to targets
    V. I will set IP Addresses and MTU value

As a senior SAN admin what precautions you should take while working on UNIX systems?

Career limiting moves

Do not list:

I. Do not Switch off the power on a UNIX system.

II. Don't name your test programs test. It's a UNIX command!

III. Don't use wildcards with rm rm *~ ,rm * ~, deletes all files.

IV. Don't give a file or program or an important file name `core'.  Many system admin scripts delete  files called `core'

V. On a crash UNIX dumps the entire kernel image to a file called `core' and they are deleted to freeup space.)

Give a generic high level method to setup replication

I. I will install the replication software such as SRDF on storage device and nodes.
II. I will create new source LUNs (R1) that can be replicated.
III. I will create target LUNs (R2)
IV. R1 and R2 LUNs must be the same size
V. I will configure the replication group
VI. I will register the replicated group
VII. I will verify the configuration
VIII. I will establish a synchronized pair of devices such as SRDF, connected by FC or IP links.

IX. A local source device is paired with a remote target device while data replication is taking place.

X. While the SRDF devices are paired, the remote target device is not locally accessible for read or writes operations.
XI. When the data replication operation completes, the pair may be split to enable normal read/write access to both devices.
XII. The pair may be restored to restore the data on the local source device

What is a World Wide Name (WWN)?

A World Wide Name, or WWN, is a 64-bit address used in fibre channel networks to uniquely identify each element in a Fibre Channel network. Soft Zoning utilizes World Wide Names to assign security permissions.

The use of World Wide Names for security purposes is inherently insecure, because the World Wide Name of a device is a user-configurable parameter.

For example, to change the World Wide Name (WWN) of an Emulex HBA, the users simply need to run the `elxcfg` command.

WWN = World Wide Name
WWPN = World Wide Port Name
WWNN = World Wide Node Name.

WWPN is the number reference the traffic to a particular port of the HBA.
WWNN is for whole HBA. If it's a dual port HBA connecting to the SAN, WWPN must be used.

What are the classes of attacks against SANs?

Snooping, Spoofing, Denial of Service.

What is FCAP (Fibre Channel Authentication Protocol)?

FCAP is an optional authentication mechanism employed between any two devices or entities on a Fibre Channel network using certificates or optional keys.

Why the actual size of disk is less than logical size?

Because manufactures use the following for

Physical storage capacity:

1 kilobyte (KB) = 1,000 bytes
1 megabyte (MB) = 1,0002 bytes
1 gigabyte (GB) = 1,0003 bytes
1 terabyte (TB) = 1,0004 bytes
1 petabyte (PB) = 1,0005 bytes

Where as logical capacity is based on Base 2

Logical storage capacity: Base 2

1 KB = 1,024 bytes
1 MB = 1,024 KB or 1,024^2 bytes
1 GB = 1,024 MB or 1,024^3 bytes
1 TB = 1,024 GB or 1,024^4 bytes
1 PB = 1,024 TB or 1,024^5 bytes
1 block = 512 bytes

Explain various connectivity options for long distance?

	Dark Fibre	CWDM	DWDM	SONET/SDH	IP
Distance in KM	40	100	200	1000	Unlimited
Latency in us/km	5	5	Low	Medium	Variable
Bandwidth in Gbps	100	8 Channels, 2.5Gbps	100 Channels 40Gbps	OC-192 10Gbps	Variable
Cost	Low	Low	High	Medium	High

Explain PID Port Identifier Format ?

PIDs are used by the routing and zoning services in Fibre Channel fabrics to identify ports in the network.

The PID is a 24-bit address built from three fields:
Domain,
Area_ID, and
AL_PA.

Each of the domain, area_ID, and AL_PA portions of the PID require eight bits in the address space.

What are the various components of WWWN?

WWN Formats :

   I. Vendor Unique Code
  II. Product Code
 III. Product Type
 IV. Serial Number
  V. Port Number

How to find Peak Rolling Average (PRA) in SAN?

Peak Rolling Average (PRA):

(PRA in MB/sec) x (cycle time seconds) = (Cumulative peak data change)

What are SAN 24-Bit Port Address Fields?

Bits 23-16	Bits 15-08	Bits 07-00
Domain Area	(Port)	Port (AL_PA)

What are all the SHARE Recovery Tiers?

    I. Tier 0: No off-site data – Possibly no recovery
   II. Tier 1: Data backup with no hot site
  III. Tier 2: Data backup with a hot site
  IV. Tier 3: Electronic vaulting
   V. Tier 4: Point-in-time copies
  VI. Tier 5: Transaction integrity
 VII. Tier 6: Zero or near-Zero data loss
VIII. Tier 7: Highly automated, business integrated solution

How will you define various systems availability?

System Availability: Availability = Uptime/ (Uptime + Downtime)

Availability	Downtime
I. 99%	3.65 days a year.
II. 99.9%	8.76 hours a year.
III. 99.99%	52.56 minutes a year.
IV. 99.999%	5.26 minutes a year.

Explain ROI, RTO and RPO?

Return on Investment (ROI):
ROI = (Net Profit / Cost of Investment) x 100
Total Cost Of Ownership (TCO): It incorporates hardware and software costs, installation and license tracking, warranties and maintenance agreements.

RPO= Maximum tolerable data loss (time since last backup)
RTO=Time needed from failure to recover and resume to business

How will you be replicating a database so that it may be easier to restore?

I will create four different logical volumes and replicate them:

    I. Database binaries,
   II. Data files,
  III. Logs, and
  IV. Meta data files

Why you use block level storage systems?

In the block level storage, I can create raw volumes of storage and each block can be controlled as an individual hard drive.
Block level storage data transportation is much efficient and reliable.
Block level storage can be used to store files as well as provide the storage required for special applications like Databases, VMFS etc.

What Buffer to Buffer Credits for Long Distances you recommend?

I.	1 gigabit	0.5 credit per kilometer
II.	2 gigabit	1 credit per kilometer
III.	4 gigabit	2 credits per kilometer

What kind of SAN deployments have you done?

1. <u>Fibre Channel SAN</u>

I have designed Fibre Channel SAN , Providing Fibre Channel (FC) host connections with all the operating systems-Windows®, ESX Server, Solaris™, Oracle® Enterprise Linux®, Red Hat Linux, SUSE Linux, AIX, HP/UX, NetWare, and OpenVMS.

I have used Fibre Channel Technology as it supports speed up to 16 GB/s, it's highly scalable; and it can accommodate approx 15 million devices.

To make best use of the available bandwidth between switches, I use ISL trunking on all ISLs.

2. <u>IP SAN</u>

I have also implemented IP SAN by carrying SCSI commands over IP networks: iSCSI SAN solution using Ethernet IP protocols from 1Gb to 10Gb. IP SAN uses TCP as a transport mechanism for storage over Ethernet, and iSCSI encapsulates SCSI commands into TCP packets, thus enabling the transport of I/O block data over IP networks. With Fibre Channel IP or iSCSI connections, it is best to use jumbo frames in the IP network.

I. Internet Storage Name Service (iSNS) is a software component that registers the presence of iSCSI initiators and targets on a SAN and responds to queries from iSNS clients.

II. iSCI initiator is a hardware or software device running on a computer that accesses the storage devices on the SAN.

III. iSCI target is a component integrated into a drive array or computer that receives SCSI command from the initiator and passes the to a storage device.

Can you explain the structure and organization of FC Data?

The Fibre Channel protocol transmits data in frames each of which can contain up to 2112 bytes of payload data.

Frame is the fundamental unit of data transfer; consists of five parts:

1. SOF
2. Frame header
3. data field
4. CRC and
5. EOC

Explain how you do block level storage virtualization?

I use block level storage virtualization to provide virtualization layer in SAN.
I create a storage pool by aggregating luns by abstracting block storage devices.
Then I put a virtualization appliance that forms virtual volumes from storage pools and then I assign LUNs to hosts.

VSAN- logical fabric on a FC SAN enabling communication among a group of nodes, regardless of their physical location in the fabric

Virtual Provisioning provides virtualization of LUNs at the storage system level. A virtually provisioned LUN is called a thin LUN (TLU). A thin LUN presents more capacity to an application than is physically available. Additional capacity on a thin

For virtualization I have used:

VPLEX from EMC
USPV and VSP from HITACHI

What you like about storage virtualization?

I like online volume expansion and non disruptive migration.

I can non-disruptively and automatically add LUN from a reserve storage pool.

Explain the use of Datagram

I. A Class 3 Fibre Channel service that allows data to be sent quickly to multiple devices attached to the fabric, with no confirmation of receipt.

II. Class 3 service in Fibre Channel is analogous to datagram service such as UDP/IP in LAN environments.

III. Frames are streamed from initiator to target with no acknowledgment of receipt.

For example: I have used port 138 on NAS for UDP:

138   UDP   NETBIOS Datagram Service   Needed for CIFS.

How does FSPF work?

I. Fabric Shortest Path First.
II. Its algorithm shaping traffic management on switches.
III. It takes shortest route first.
IV. FSPF keeps track of the state of the links on all switches in the Fabric and associates a cost with each link.

What can you do to fix zoning information in FibreZone database?

I will use Refresh Zoning to push the changes out to the switch(es)/fabric:

fzone fabric –refresh

Explain the difference between "In-Band" and "Out-of-Band" Virtualization?

I. In-band: When we implement an in-band virtual storage network, both data and control flow over the same path.

II. Out-of-band: the data flow is separated from the control flow. This is done by separating the data and meta-data into different places.

What kind of disks you recommend for various types of data?

I. Tier 1: mission-critical data that requires high availability and fast access. Mission critical refers to system whose failure will result in the failure of business operations. I will use 15k fc or sas disk drives for such applications. The dual-port point-to-point sas interface provides highest reliability (1.6m hour mtbf) and performance: high iops (input/output operations per second), mb/second throughput.

II. Tier 2: data that requires fast, but not the fastest access. I will use Nearline, 5.4K and 7.2K rpm drives; Nearline SAS and Enterprise SATA drives

III. Tier 3: I will use this tier for static, rarely accessed data. Such as backup. Tape libraries and Emerging Technologies.

IV. Tier 0: I will use Solid-State Drive (SSD) Technology for time-sensitive or mission-critical data that requires the fastest data storage. Its good for random I/O (input/output). For example Database environments have very active files with high write I/Os.

Explain the Structure of Storage department and roles and responsibilities?

Director or Manager of Storage Group

Responsibilities:

I. Gather requirements
II. Select the appropriate topology and solutions based on end-user requirements.
III. Plan and design fabric solutions based on best practices
IV. Migration from old to new SAN
V. Plan for growth
VI. Identify tools and techniques used for planning and design.
VII. Create a logical and physical SAN design.
VIII. Implement storage solutions throughout the life cycle of a project.
IX. Provide training and mentoring

Storage Project Manager

Responsibilities:

I. Manages deliverables towards the initiatives timeframes
II. Select the appropriate level of SAN support
III. Works to insure process compliance with other Data Center support groups
IV. Capacity planning for continual growth and expansion based on customer requirements.

Lead Storage Engineer

Responsibilities:
I. Leadership and core skill for SAN environment
II. Documentation, testing, and integration of SAN management
III. SAN configuration, installation, documentation
IV. Modifications and growth plans related to the SAN environment
V. Technical review
VI. Capacity planning
VII. Monitor storage and utilization performance.
VIII. Technical mentoring of Storage Administrators and technicians

Storage Engineer Technical Lead

Responsibilities:
I. Design of large scale SAN infrastructure, storage frames
II. Keep extensive knowledge of contemporary SAN technologies
III. Configuration and administration of the Storage environment

Storage Network Administrator

Responsibilities:

Administration and Maintenance

I. Day-to-day implementation and configuration of systems within the SAN, Fibre Channel Host Bus Adapter and Drivers, Host Bus Adapter LUN Masking, Storage LUN Masking, Fibre Channel Switch Administration
II. Software upgrades
III. SAN trouble shooting

Switch Fabric Administration

I. Software upgrades
II. Firmware upgrades
III. License Management
IV. Backup Switch Configuration

Storage Frame Administration

I. Software upgrades
II. Firmware upgrades
III. License Management
IV. Storage Reconfiguration

What type of fabric mode you must set your switches to?

Open Fabric mode

How you Discover device names of LUNs on an HP-UX server?

Enter the following commands to create special device files:

ioscan -fnC disk
insf -e

How will you calculate raw capacity?

Raw Capacity= Usable + Parity

What is a Meta Device?

Meta Devices Meta devices allow individual devices to be concatenated to create larger devices. The Meta head is the first device in the Meta device sequence and is responsible for receiving incoming commands.

What is used for Device Masking?

Storage arrays Device Masking, devices that have been masked for visibility to certain hosts. The device masking database which holds device masking records, typically resides on a small disk device (such as a 16 cylinder, 8 MB device).

You are a SAN Admin and Users are complaining about performance how can you see the performance statistics?

Counters on each storage arrays unit accumulate event hits and status of certain operations. Using Storage Vendors Tools we can see performance statistics for:
  I. The entire storage arrays
  II. One or all directors of a specified type
  III. A device
  IV. A device group
  V. Disks
  VI. Mirrors
  VII. LRU cache management entities.

What is an HBA?

Host Bus Adapters. Fibre Channel host bus adapters live in the servers, and provide the connection to the SAN's hubs and switches. They come with HSC or PCI interfaces, single or double ports, and replaceable Gigabit Link Modules (GLMs) or Gigabit Interface Controllers (GBICs). Fibre Channel HBAs are usually based on AgilentTechnologies' Tachyon or TachLite chip.

Fibre Channel Host Bus Adapters (HBAs) are similar to the SCSI HBAs and NICs.

Typically, HBA uses the PCI bus and has an integrated component that handles all the Fibre Channel protocol processing.

What are the ways to manage Brocade switch?

Telnet, Webtools

Explain Fibre Channel logins?

Fibre Channel logins takes place after a link is operational. There are three different types of logins in Fibre Channel technology

   I.   Fabric Login (FLOGI)
  II.   Port Login (PLOGI)
 III.   Process Login (PRLI)

What information is passed during PLOGI?

WWN, S_ID, ULP, Class, BB Credit. N_Port to N_Port

What information is passed during PRLI?

LUN #. Communicated by the ULP (SCSI-3 to SCSI-3)

Explain FLOGI?

(FLOGI) process allows a node to log in to the fabric
The information passed during FLOGI: WWN, S_ID, Protocol, Class, and Zoning. N_Port to F_Port

What you use to avoid storage device corruption in vCenter Server?

I will use vCenter Server Storage Filtering. They are:

I. VMFS Filter;
II. RDM Filter;
III. Same Host and Transports Filter;
IV. Host Rescan Filter

Explain fabric merge? How to do it?

It's connecting multiple switches together.

I. Assign Unique domain IDs on all switches
II. I will rename the zone sets so they look similar on both the switches.
III. Even a zone on each switch with same name but different members will result in failure. I will make sure the zone names are unique.
IV. The R_A_TOV and E_D_TOV values must be the same on all switches.
V. The InteropMode setting must be identical on all switches.
VI. I will now ISL the switches and the zone sets will merge automatically.

You got a failed fibre switch what actions you will take?

I. I will order a replacement switch.
II. I will clean all the zoning information on the replacement switch.
III. Then I will Change the Domain ID of the replacement switch to the domain ID of the old switch

How will you secure a fibre switch management?

I will use a separate management LAN
A separate, VLAN-based management access

Explain your experience with dynamic disk

Windows Server 2008 provides the alternative to the basic disk type.
Dynamic disks can have an unlimited number of volumes using various configurations. I can create volumes that can be stored on multiple disks, create mirrored disks or even a combination between those two.

To perform disk management tasks in Windows Server 2008?

DiskPart.exe

Is it possible to setup an ISL between Cisco and Brocade switches?

Yes.

I will configure Cisco and Brocade interoperability. For a Mixed vendor fabric expansion all switches that partake in the interoperable VSAN should have that VSAN set to interop mode, even if they do not have any end devices.

Explain your experience with disk duplexing

Duplexing adds another disk controller.
It's a fault tolerance mechanism in which the computer stores duplicate data on two separate disks, each on a separate host adapter, so that the data remains available if one disk fails.

Explain your experience with logical unit number (LUN)

LUN is an identifier assigned to a specific component within a SCSI device, such as an individual disk drive in an array, which enables the SCSI host adapter to send commands to that component.

Explain your experience with VDS hardware provider?

I.   VDS is a software component that enables to use the Storage Manager for SANs snap-in to manage LUNs on an external storage device.

II. VDS provides application programming interfaces (API) used to manage storage hardware, discover and configure resources for storage devices with a unified interface.

III. I have used VDS for common storage management tasks such as creating LUNs, extending existing LUNs, connecting LUNs to hosts within the storage area network (SAN), and inventorying storage resources.

What is use of Fibre Channel Link Services?

I.   Fibre Channel Link Services defines Registered State Change Notifications (RSCNs).
II. It's used for notifying Nx_Ports that are registered to receive them with timely indications of changes to nodes attached to the fabric.
III. The single channel transfer rate is 106 MB/second (1 gigabit/sec)

Fibre Channel is an American National Standards Institute (ANSI) interface that acts as a general transport vehicle to simultaneously deliver the command sets of which protocols?

SCSI-3, IPI-3, HIPPI-FP, IP, and ATM/AAL5.

What Replication Modes you are familiar with?

I have used two modes of data replication:

   I. Synchronous replication
  II. Asynchronous replication

How you manage Fiber Channel?

     I. Common Transport (FC-CT) In band Management
    II. IP over FC In-band Management
   III. WEB Based Management Out of Band Management
   IV. SNMP Standardized Out of Band Management
    V. Telnet/CLI Out of Band Management
   VI. API Based Management Out of Band Management

What transmission you will use to fully utilize available bandwidth?

I will use asynchronous transmission to fully utilize the available bandwidth.
Write operation is confirmed as complete before the remote volume has been updated.

Explain the use of ordered sets?

The Ordered Sets are 4 byte transmission words containing data and special characters which have a special meaning.
Ordered Sets provide the availability to obtain bit and word synchronization.

There are three primary categories of ordered sets:

   I. Primitive signals
  II. Primitive sequences
  III. Frame delimiters

Explain CIM and SMI-S

   I. The Common Information Model (CIM) is an open standard that defines how managed elements in an IT environment are represented as a common set of objects and relationships between them.

II. CIM provides the mechanism to actively control and manage the elements.

III. Storage Management Initiative Specification (SMI-S): SMI-S is based on the Common Information Model (CIM) and the Web-Based Enterprise Management (WBEM) standards, management functionality via HTTP.

How many parts CIM have?

I. The CIM Specification
II. CIM Schema

A user wants to access block-oriented and file based disks of the same storage system, what can you do?

I have used convergence via HNAS supporting NFS and CIFS and providing access to files on the Storage Array.

Explain ASIC?

ASIC: Application Specific Integrated Circuit is a non-standard integrated circuits that have been designed for a specific use or application. For example Brocade designs its Fibre Channel ASICs for performing switching functions in its SAN switches.

Year 1997: Brocade's first Fibre Channel switch SilkWorm 1000 used "Stitch" ASIC.

Year 2001 to 2003, Brocade Fibre Channel switches based on its third generation ASIC, "BLOOM"

The fifth generation of ASICs, called Condor and Golden eye:

I. 4G: Condor and Golden Eye

II. 8G: Condor2 and GoldenEye2

III. 16G: Condor3

Explain FPGA?

Field-programmable gate arrays (FPGA): It uses programmable logic blocks and programmable interconnects to allow the same FPGA to be used in many different applications. They can be used to implement any logical function.

For example:

Hitachi in its HNAS implements pipelined network file operations via its Silicon File System FPGA-based server architecture. It uses many FPGAs to implement network, file system and storage operations.

Which port is used by the SAN (Storage Area Network) incorporating SCSI drivers without the need of attaching extra disks?

iSCSI uses TCP as its transport protocol.
The well known TCP port for iSCSI traffic is 3260.

What is RDM? What kind of LUN you need for RDM?

I use Raw Disk Mapping (RDM) to present a LUN directly to a virtual machine from a SAN. It's useful for any application running in a virtual machine that needs to access a device using hardware-specific SCSI commands.

Rather than creating a virtual disk (VMDK) on a LUN.
The RDM allows a virtual machine to directly access and use the storage device.
The RDM contains metadata for managing and redirecting disk access to the physical device.
To create raw device mapping the LUN must be an unassigned raw LUN.

How do you view SAN disks using Logical Volume Management?

Logical Volume Management gives flexibility with disk management.
Disks and partitions can be abstracted to contain multiple disks and partitions into one device

I use these commands on various platforms/ LVMs:

   I. Solaris# format

FORMAT MENU:
    disk   - select a disk
    type   - select (define) a disk type
    partition - select (define) a partition table
    current   - describe the current disk
    format   - format and analyze the disk
    fdisk   - run the fdisk program (x86 only)
    repair   - repair a defective sector
    label   - write label to the disk
    analyze   - surface analysis
    defect   - defect list management
    backup   - search for backup labels
    verify   - read and display labels
    save   - save new disk/partition definitions
    inquiry   - show vendor, product and revision
    volname   - set 8-character volume name
    !<cmd>   - execute <cmd>, then return
    quit

disk

Command

Lists all of the system's drives. Also lets you choose the disk you want to use in subsequent operations. This disk is referred to as the current disk.

   II. AIX# lsdev; smit

lsdev Command
Purpose

Displays devices in the system and their characteristics.
Syntax

lsdev [-C][-c Class] [-s Subclass] [-t Type] [-f File] [-F Format | -r ColumnName] [-h] [-H] [-l { Name | - }] [-p Parent] [-S State] [start of change-xend of change]

lsdev -P [-c Class] [-s Subclass] [-t Type] [-f File] [-F Format | -r ColumnName] [-h] [-H] [start of change-xend of change]
Description

The lsdev command displays information about devices in the Device Configuration database.

III.   HP-UX# ioscan –fnC disk

ioscan(1M)   ioscan(1M)

NAME
    ioscan - scan I/O system

SYNOPSIS
    /usr/sbin/ioscan [-k | -u] [-d driver | -C class] [-I instance]
        [-H hw_path] [-f[-n] | -F[-n]] [devfile]

Linux#lvmdiskscan

lvmdiskscan - scan for all devices visible to LVM2
Synopsis
lvmdiskscan [-d | --debug] [-h | -? | --help] [-l | --lvmpartition] [-v | --verbose]
Description
lvmdiskscan scans all SCSI, (E) IDE disks, multiple devices and a bunch of other block devices in the system looking for LVM physical volumes.

IV.   Veritas#vxdisk list

What you need for Brocade switches to login?

IP, username, password

Tell us SAN Design Lifecycle?

It has 6 phases:
    I.   Data collection
    II.   Data analysis
    III. Architecture development
    IV. Prototype and test
    V.   Release to production
    VI. Maintenance

How to perform performance analysis in a SAN Environment?

I will start with *IN-DEPTH LOOK AT THE I/O DATA PATH FROM THE APPLICATION THROUGH THE OPERATING SYSTEM*, Also SAN Storage performance analysis must be used in conjunction with all the other components like:

    I. OS
    II. Database
    III. Application, and
    IV. Network

So it's important for SAN Administrator to learn about all the components.

What Methods have you used to improve cache performance?

I have used cache partitioning.
Cache partitioning is used to logically divide the Array cache.
Devices are assigned to a partition and can only use the cache they have been assigned. This way the workloads that are cache friendly can be guaranteed more cache resources, increasing the aggregate cache utilization

Give some examples of HBAs?

Emulex LP8000, LP952, LP9002, LP982, LP9802, LP9802DC, LP10000.

Fig: Emulex HBA

Explain Fibre Channel Protocols?

Connection-oriented services
Class 1   with acknowledgment, full bandwidth
Class 4   Virtual connections, Quos,
           fractional bandwidth
Class 6   Uni-directional
Connectionless services
Class 2   With acknowledgment
Class 3   Without acknowledgment

Node levels

FC-4 Translation between Fibre Channel and
       command sets that use it: HiPPI, SCSI, IPI,
       SBCCS, IP, IEEE 802.2, audio, video
FC-3 Common services across multiple ports
Port levels (FC-PH standard)
FC-2 Framing and flow control
FC-1 8B/10B encoding, error detection
FC-0 Electrical and optical characteristics

Name Basic SAN Components?

A SAN will have the following basic components:

   I. HBA (Host Bus Adapter)

II.   Fibre/Copper Cabling
III. Fibre Channel Switch
IV. Fibre Attached Array
V.   Management System

How to update Linux OS when you install a new hardware such as HBA?

I will modify modprobe.conf file and run mkinitrd

How will you allow LINUX to see more than 0 LUNs?

I will edit Linux modprobe.conf file.

I will edit the /etc/modprobe.conf file to allow the Fibre Channel HBA driver to scan for LUNs greater than 0.

    options scsi_mod max_luns=255

Make a backup of original kernel file.
    #mv /boot/initrd-linux_kernel_version.img
    /boot/initrd-linux_kernel_version.img.bak

Run The mkinitrd script. It generates the initrd image that is loaded by the bootloader and executed by the kernel during boot

    #mkinitrd -v /boot/initrd-linux_kernel_version.img
    linux_kernel_version

Explain Fibre Channel technology options nomenclature   100-SM-LL-L?

100	SM	LL	L
Speed (MB/sec)	Media	Transmitter	Distance

400 = 400 MB/sec | SM = Single Mode | LL = Longwave Laser | L = Long

200 = 200 MB/sec | M5 = Multimode (50um) | SL = Shortwave Laser w OFC | I = Intermediate

100 = 100 MB/sec | M6 = Multimode (62,5um) | SN = Shortwave Laser w/o OFC | S = Short

50 = 50 MB/sec | TV = Video Cable | LE = Longwave LED

| MI = Miniature Cable | EL = Electrical

| TP = Twisted Pair

What are different SAN Topologies?

SAN makes use of three kinds of topologies in its configuration:
Point-to-point, arbitrated loop, and switched.

When these three topologies are interconnected, a fabric is created. Point-to-point is a simple and easily applied topology for connecting two nodes, and the bandwidth is dedicated to these two nodes. A connection between a storage device and a server uses point-to-point topology. The point-to-point connectivity is also applicable between two CPUs. This type of topology is best used on a small scale. The loop (arbitrated) topology ensures that the bandwidth is shared between all the nodes that are connected to the loop, unlike point-to-point topology. The loop can also be connected node-to-node, but this might cause the loop to stop functioning if even one node malfunctions. The arbitrated loop is cost-effective in terms of the high bandwidth and connectivity it offers. The arbitrated-loop technology can support up to 126 nodes. It is possible to connect a loop to a Fibre Channel switch to further increase a fabric's size.

Explain different Fibre Channel Ports?

There are three basic types of ports: the N_Port, the F_Port, and the E_Port.

I. N_Port
An N_Port is a node port, or a port on a disk or computer. If a port is only an N_Port (and not an NL_Port), it can communicate only with another N_Port on a second node or to an F_Port on a switch.

II. F_Port

An F_Port is a fabric port, which is found only on a switch. If a port is only an F_Port (and not an FL_Port), it can connect only to another N_Port via a point-to point connection.

III. L_Port

An L_Port implies it can participate in an arbitrated loop. If a port was only an L_Port, it could connect only to arbitrated loops, but ports that are exclusively L_Ports don't exist. The L is added to the end of an N_Port or F_Port to create an NL_Portor an FL_Port.

IV. NL_Port
A node port with arbitrated loop capabilities; that is, a port on a node that can connect to another node, to a switch (see N_Port) or to an arbitrated loop

V. FL_Port
A fabric port with arbitrated loop capabilities; that is, a port on a switch that can connect to a node (see F_Port) or an arbitrated loop

VI. E_Port
An E_Port is an expansion port on a switch that connects one switch to other switches via their E_Ports to form a large fabric.

VII. G_Port

A G_Port is a generic port on a switch that can act as an E_Port, an FL_Port, or an F_Port, depending on what connects to it.

What is World Wide Name (WWN)?

Used to identify entities such as ports
64-bit address
Fixed factory assigned or software generated address
Made of WWPN and WWNN

A worldwide name has two components: a Worldwide Port name (WWPN) and a Worldwide node name (WWNN). The WWNN can be used to identify a unit containing a group of ports. The WWNN is neither universally nor consistently used by the industry. A host may have one WWNN for the entire unit, but several
WWPNs (one for each port). A WWN consists of eight hex pairs separated by colons, for example 10:00:08:00:88:44:50: ef

What is Inter-Switch Link (ISL)?

Used to expand fabric connectivity
Switches communicate with each other using ISLs to:
Transfer host to storage data
Transfer fabric management traffic host.

What is ISL Trunking?

Trunking is aggregation of ISLs to Prevent Link Congestion.
It provides the ability to aggregate multiple physical links into one logical link for enhanced network performance and fault tolerance.

Do you know Zoning Best Practices?

It should be Single HBA Zoning:
A separate zone should be created for each HBA
Makes zone management easier when replacing HBAs Storage ports or HBAs can be members of multiple zones

There are three types of zones:
Port Zoning (Hard Zoning)
WWN based Zoning (Soft Zoning)
Hybrid zones that can contain ports and WWNs (Mixed Zoning)

Name Basic SAN Components?

A SAN will have the following basic components:
HBA (Host Bus Adapter)
Fibre/Copper Cabling
Fibre Channel Switch
Fibre Attached Array
Management System

Define Replication?

It provides comprehensive business continuity and restart capabilities for both planned and unplanned outages. This online, host-independent, mirrored data solution duplicates production site data on one or more physically separate target storage arrays systems. Systems can be across the room, across the globe, or anywhere in between.

Explain how will you perform replication for HDS arrays?

According to HDS products releases,

I. Hitachi Universal Replicator for asynchronous replication over any distance Hitachi TrueCopy for synchronous
II. TC is push based replication, HUR is pull based.
III. Hitachi Universal Replicator software on the DR or secondary storage array pulls data from cache on the primary storage array.
IV. Asynchronous: Stores time-stamped IO packets in the primary disk array and transfers them to the secondary array subject to link bandwidth.
V. Synchronous each write to the primary volume to be performed to the secondary as well
VI. Truecopy maximum distance of 300km.
VII. Universal Replicator primary and secondary volumes can be any distance from each other.

What Types of Configuration are possible with Replication?

Three types of configuration: Uni-directional, Bi-directional, and Dual Configuration.
Uni-directional is a one way mirror relationship.
Bi-directional is a two-way mirror relationship.
Dual Configuration is two uni-directional configurations.

Explain how will you setup HUR Replication?

I. First I will setup replication paths between arrays,

II. I will setup ports as Initiators on the array that holds the primary volumes and setup ports as RCU Targets on the arrays that hold the remote volumes.

III. I will identify the parity groups that will be used for replication on both arrays

IV. I will specify the journal volumes.

V. I will Configure Command Devices

VI. I will setup HORCM config, config file per storage array

How will you identify and find a command device in Hitachi SAN?

As per HDS products manual:

I. Raidscan command shows volumes specification
II. raidscan -x findcmddev hdisk0,100

How will you manage HDS Array replication by using CLI?

I will use the following command from HDS products manual:

The **pairdisplay** command displays the pairing status.

I. To display the pair status: pairdisplay

II. To create the pair: paicreate

III. To split the pair: pairsplit

IV. To Resync the split pairs: pairresync

Explain Inflow Control?

I. It allows a reduction in the number of I/Os by delaying the response to the host I/Os
II. Inflow control –Off is the normal mode

III. If I have to maintain application response time, I will disable it

Explain what is the various Volume statuses in HDS replication?

I. SMPL simplex
II. PAIR paired
III. COPY copying
IV. PSUS Pair Suspended
V. SSUS Secondary Suspended
VI. PSUE Pair suspend – error
VII. PSUF Pair Full Sidefile
VIII. PFUS PFUS is PSUS with reason of sidefile full

Name Hitachi HDS storage array which supports virtualization?

I. Hitachi Virtual Storage Platform (VSP).
II. Hitachi Unified Storage VM (HUS VM).
III. Hitachi Unified Storage (HUS) 100

Explain the architecture of HDS VSP array?

I. FED Front end Director =>host interface
II. BED Back end Director => disk interface
III. VSD:Virtual Storage Directors => central processor boards
IV. DCA:Cache Memory Adapter => memory boards (cache) for read/write data
V. GSW:Grid Switch => HiStar E Network, PCI-Express switch system

How will you monitor HDS, Hitachi Storage Arrays?

Hi-Track Remote Monitoring, Hi-Track supports all the HDS products

Explain the functions of SVP?

I. The laptop runs the Service Processor (SVP) as the primary configuration user interface.
II. I can use SVP to perform most configuration tasks and for monitoring & reporting

What is HDT?

I. Hitachi Dynamic Tiering is optimizing data placement in tier 1, 2, or 3
II. Pages that do not remain hot enough or competitive will demote
III. HDT is possible only on VSP.

Explain the use of HDP?

I. It spreads host I/O patterns across many physical disks.
II. Basic allocation unit 42MB

When will you use CLPR?

I. CLPR allows to partition cache.

II. Assignment of a specific data cache to parity groups assigned to that cache allocation.

III. Total no. of CLPR=32

When will you enable Port Security?

For connecting multiple servers with different operating systems to the same port

How will you prevent illegal access of a LUN, when sharing?

  I. I will enable LUN security on ports, this will allow me to add multiple WWNs to one Host Group,

  II. Add a LDEV to two different Host Groups on the same FC port,

  III. Create host groups with different Host connection modes on the same FC port.

What is a FAN in Ratio?

A maximum number of storage ports can be access by single initiator or host

Which protocol is used in windows to share file?

CIFS

iSCSI naming uses which service?

iSNS
Internet Storage Name Service (iSNS) is needed to facilitate the discovery and configuration of iSCSI devices it uses port 3205.

Users complain about slow file transfers on a SUN server with an Emulex HBA. How to check the settings of the HBA?

#lputil

lputil help: will show a list of lputil commands

Which file control the ability on a Sun Solaris host to see the disks?

sd.conf

What is sd.conf?

Its Solaris' SCSI driver configuration files, /kernel/drv/sd.conf,

How to add a disk to a Sun Solaris host online?

Drvconfig, disks, devlinks

How to view disk usage in UNIX?

du - disk usage
du - report disk usage in "blocks" (512 bytes)
du - k - report disk usage in kilobytes

What is the 64-bit hardware address for a Fibre Channel HBA?

World Wide Name, WWWN

Name a few Cisco MDS 9000 products?

Cisco MDS 9020 Series Fabric Switches
Cisco MDS 9100 Series Multilayer Fabric Switches
Cisco MDS 9200 Series Multilayer Fabric Switches
Cisco MDS 9500 Series Multilayer Directors

Which MDS-9000 director is capable of supporting the emerging 10 Gb bandwidth?

9509

Fig: Cisco MDS 9000 Series Multilayer Switch

Which native command on a B-series switch provides data for troubleshooting?

supportshow

What unique ID is assigned to a SAN Switch?

Manually assign a unique domain ID prior to adding a switch to an existing fabric.

Explain the difference between initiator-based and mutual CHAP authentication?

Initiator CHAP validates the initiator secret against the one stored on the array.
Mutual CHAP is a bi-directional authentication.

What is LUN Trespass?

Its Storage Port Failover, it enables the move of LUNs, on an active port failure, from the active to the passive port

What are the CHAP security levels?

One-way CHAP authentication. With this level of security, only the target authenticates the initiator.

Mutual CHAP authentication. With this level of security, the target and the initiator authenticate each other.

IPsec. With this level of security, all IP packets sent during data transfers are encrypted and authenticated

How to discover newly added LUNs on HP-UX?

ioscan -fnc disk

Explain SAN Virtualization?

Essentially   SAN Virtualization   means having an appliance in the data path that can take physical storage from one or more storage subsystems and present it to hosts in the form of a virtual disk (VDisk)

How to force the host to perform a Fabric login to a switch in an Emulex HBA Solaris host installation?

lpfc.conf

FC_AL tape drive to a fibre channel switch was connected.

How the switches identify the drive, during FLOGI?

NL_port

How to mount and assign the LUN On the HP-UX Backup server?

    I.   Vgimport
   II.   vgchange -a y /dev/<volume group>
  III.   fsck -F vxfs /dev/<volume group>/<logical volume>
  IV.   Mount the file system.

What are the options in lputil?

1. List Adapters
2. Adapter Information
3. Firmware Maintenance
4. Reset Adapter

What is HBAnywhere?

HBAnyware is the GUI version of Emulex's configuration tool lputil

Define Some Media Protection-RAIDs that can be configured?

Data protection options are configured at the volume level and the same system can employ a variety of protection schemes

Mirroring (RAID 1)

Highest performance, availability and functionality, two mirrors of one storage arrays Logical Volume located on separate physical drives

Parity RAID
3 +1 (3 data and 1 parity volume) or 7 +1 (7 data and 1 parity volume)

RAID 10 – Mirrored Stripped Mainframe Volumes

RAID 6 can handle the failure of any two drives in the array
Because of two sets of parity information.

What are the advantages of using a RAID-10? When to use?

    I. High write throughputs
   II. Sustain multiple drive failures
I will use it for data backup operations.

What is Dynamic Sparing?

One or more HDDs that are used when storage arrays detects a potentially failing (or failed) device Can be utilized to augment data protection scheme
Minimizes exposure after a drive failure and before drive replacement

How you discover LUNs on AIX?

Use cfgmgr command
How to discover new LUN on Sun Solaris?

Run devfsadm -C. This will re-check the HBAs for connections.
Run powercf -q, powermt config, and
 "Powermt display dev=all" to see whether the new LUN shows up.

If it does not work:
Perform a reboot reconfigure (reboot -- -r).

How to discover new disks on Linux?

Linux currently do not have kernel command like drvconfig or ioscan. For a dynamic SCSI channel reconfiguration so do one of the following:

- I. Reboot the host
- II. Unload and load the HBA driver
- III. Echoing the SCSI device list in /proc
- IV. Execute a SCSI scan exposed to /sys
- V. Execute a SCSI scan function through HBA vendor scripts

How to extend a file system on Linux?

- I. Perform a backup of existing file system.
- II. Unmount the file system.
- III. Increase the size of the SAN disk.
- IV. sfdisk -R to re-read the new partition size.
- V. fdisk to remove, recreate the new larger partition. e2fsck.
- VI. e2fsck.
- VII. resize2fs.
- VIII. Mount your newly resized file system.

How to extend an uncounted ReiserFS file system?

resize_reiserfs -s +size G device

If a SUN Host cannot see disks, what can you do?

Some times the problem is caused by the incorrect settings in HBA configuration file lpfc.conf and system (SCSI) device configuration file sd.conf. To make the SUN host recognizes the storage arrays devices (disks); set the recommended parameters in lpfc.conf and sd.conf

You assigned LUNs from a Storage array and Veritas volume manager on a host sees too many LUNs or ghost LUNs, what could be the reason?

It happens when ASL - Array Support Library from Veritas is missing.
I will fix it by installing ASL - Array Support Library from Veritas with latest patches.

Explain IPC and Semaphores? How you can tune system?

You may be able to improve IPC performance by tuning the configuration attributes.

Inter Process Communication is a UNIX mechanism whereby processes communicate with one another. The communication is done via a number of facilities. These are primarily shared memory segments, messages queues and semaphores.

To display information about active inter-process communication facilities, you can use the '/usr/bin/ipcs' command.

To display information about active shared memory segments, the 'ipcs -m' command can be used.

To display information about active message queues, the 'ipcs -q' command can be used.

To display information about active semaphores, the 'ipcs -s can be used.
To display information about all active IPC facilities, use 'ipcs -a'

To query the Solaris kernel for current IPC settings, i.e. maximum number of identifiers, etc, the Solaris '/usr/sbin/sysdef' command can be used. This will list kernel settings for messages, semaphores and shared memory.

To remove IPC entries, the '/usr/bin/ipcrm' command may be used. This takes as an argument either the key or the ID of the facility you wish to remove. The key & ID can be retrieved from the 'ipcs -a' command.

What is iSCSI?

iSCSI stands for internet SCSI, or internet Small Computer Systems Interface.

iSCSI is the transmission of SCSI commands and data over IP networks.

A host cannot be connected to both iSCSI and a Fibre channel storage system. Furthermore, while an iSCSI array may be capable of accepting connections from HBAs and NICs, a host cannot have both NIC and HBA connections to an iSCSI storage system.

A host requires an iscsi software.
An iSCSI service should be running on Host.

For example:

QLogic's 4000 Series 1GbE iSCSI Adapters
It will provide SAN connectivity over Ethernet and TCP/IP network infrastructures.

Fig : QLogic's 4000 Series 1GbE iSCSI Adapters

Explain various components of iSCSI?

I. AHS: Additional Header Segment - A variable-length header that optionally follows the 48-byte Basic Header Segment in an iSCSI packet.

II. BHS: Basic Header Segment - The 48-byte header of an iSCSI packet.

III. CDB: Command Descriptor Block - The standard format for SCSI commands. CDBs are commonly 6, 10, or 12 bytes long, though they can be 16 bytes or of variable length.

IV. CHAP: Challenge Handshake Authentication Protocol - An authentication technique for confirming the identity of one computer to another. Described in RFC 1994.

V. CID: Connection Identifier - A 16-bit number, generated by the initiator, that uniquely identifies a connection between two iSCSI devices. This number is presented during the login phase.

VI. Data Digest - a code used to insure data integrity of a block of data. Checksums and CRCs are common types of digests.

VII. EUI: Extended Unique Identifier - A 64-bit number that uniquely identifies every device in the world. The format consists of 24 bits that are unique to a given company, and 40 bits assigned by the company to each device it builds.

VIII. Initiator - The originating end of a SCSI conversation. Typically a controlling device such as a computer.

IX. Inquiry - A SCSI command that reads generic information from a target device. The information returned includes device type, manufacturer, model number, and version.

X. IP: Internet Protocol - The standard Internet protocol for moving packets of information from one computer to another. Commonly combined with TCP in the phrase TCP/IP.

XI. IPS: Internet Protocol Storage - The class of protocols or devices that use the IP protocol to move data in a storage network. FCIP, iFCP, and iSCSI are all examples of IPS protocols.

XII. IQN: iSCSI Qualified Name - A name format for iSCSI that uniquely identifies every device in the world (e.g. iqn.5886.com.acme.tapedrive.sn-a12345678).

XIII. iSCSI: Internet Small Computer System Interface - a protocol for transporting SCSI commands and data across an IP network.

XIV. ISID: Initiator Session Identifier - A 48-bit number, generated by the initiator, that uniquely identifies a session between the initiator and the target. This value is created during the login process, and is sent to the target with a Login PDU.

XV. ITT: Initiator Task Tag - A 32-bit number that is unique to every outstanding command at the target. A given value of ITT can be reused once that command is complete and status has been received from the target.

XVI. Mode Select - A SCSI command that sets operating parameters on a target.

XVII. Mode Sense - A SCSI command that reads operating parameters from a target.

R2T: Ready to Transmit - The R2T PDUs are issued by the target device as buffers become available to receive more data. At the completion of the write, the target issues status and sense, indicating a successful transaction.

Network Portal - The combination of the Node's assigned IP address and the TCP port number.

PDU: Protocol Data Unit - iSCSI Protocol Data Units (PDUs) are used to send CDB commands, status, and data.

XVIII. Request Sense - A SCSI command that tells a target to return sense data (error details) back to the initiator.

XIX. SAM: SCSI Architectural Model - A document that describes the behavior of SCSI in general terms, allowing for different types of devices communicating over various media.

XX. Socket - A TCP connection established between two computers. A socket is uniquely identified by the source IP address, source port number, destination IP address, and destination port number.

XXI. SRP: Secure Remote Password - An authentication technique developed at Stanford University and described in RFC 2945.

XXII. Target - The receiving end of a SCSI conversation, typically a device such as a disk drive, tape drive, or scanner.

XXIII. Test Unit Ready - A SCSI command that checks to see if the target device is ready to read or write data to the medium.

XXIV. TOE: TCP/IP Offload Engine - A piece of hardware that implements the TCP/IP stack, and thereby "offloading" this task from the main processor. This hardware may be a custom ASIC or a network processor with firmware.

XXV. TSID: Target Session Identifier: A 16-bit number, generated by the target, that uniquely identifies a session between the initiator and the target. This value is created during the login process, and is sent to the initiator with a Login Response PDU.

XXVI. UTF-8 - A clever way of putting Unicode characters into a byte stream. If the MSB is zero, then the remaining 7 bits are interpreted as a standard ACSII character. If the MSB is one, then the lower 7 bits are combined with the next byte to create a 14-bit Unicode character.

iSCSI targets do not reconnect after a reboot. How to fix it?

This may happen if STP is enabled. To fix this:

I. Do not use spanning-tree (STP) on switch ports that connect end nodes (iSCSI initiators or storage array network interfaces); because STP typically introduces a large delay before the switch port goes into the forwarding mode

II. Use Port Fast. Port Fast reduces network interruptions that occur when devices restart.

What best practices you will follow for iSCSI?

I. Flow Control must be enabled on switches and NICs

II. Unicast storm control should be disabled on switches

III. Jumbo Frames should be enabled on switches and NICs

IV. Disable STP functionality on switch ports that connect end nodes

V. Use VLANs to separate iSCSI SAN traffic from other network traffic

What is your opinion about FCOE?

Fibre Channel over Ethernet, FCoE is a standard for using the Fibre Channel protocol over Ethernet networks.
FCoE is a protocol designed to run Fibre Channel over a 10Gb Ethernet switched environment. FCoE speeds will match all future Ethernet speeds.

Convergence Switches allows its port to toggle its identity between 16 Gb Fibre Channel and 10 Gb Ethernet. Because of this flexibility, customers can natively support Fibre Channel, FCoE, NAS and iSCSI SANs.
Qlogic has QLogic 8300 Series controllers provide 16-gigabit Fibre Channel throughput. This controller support simultaneous LAN (TCP/IP) and SAN (Fibre Channel over Ethernet (FCoE) and iSCSI) traffic at line rate, 10Gbps Ethernet (GbE) speeds.

Why will you use Fibre Channel over Ethernet (FCoE)?

The Fibre Channel portion of FCoE appears as normal Fibre Channel to a host or a switch, and therefore to a user. It is based completely on the FC model, which makes it easy to understand, manage, and troubleshoot. A major value is that FCoE uses Ethernet hardware to deliver an enterprise storage solution, while also using the existing FC management infrastructure.

The benefits of FCoE include:
   I.   Lower cabling costs by unifying to a single fabric type with less cables
   I.   Fewer adapters, switch ports, saving in power, equipment, and cooling costs
   II. Converged Network Adapter provides both Ethernet and FCoE support on a single adapter for an end-to-end solution that is easy to manage.
   III. Uses existing FC SAN administration tools
   IV. Requires no gateway
   V.   Since the FC frame is untouched, the operation is completely stateless.

What is your observation about read and writes on SSDs?

I have noticed that the write operation of SSDs is slower. The read performance of a flash chip is generally faster than that of most the disks. In order to write a block of data, the SSD's NAND Controller will first ensure that the destination block is erased. This erase/write cycle of the entire block occurs even if only a single bit changes in the block and hence writes are slower.

Explain the use of WAN Optimization Controller (WOC)?

It is a network appliance that enhances WAN performance by accelerating long-distance TCP/IP communications.

What is a Simplex volume?

Simplex volumes accept Read/ Write I/Os.

What is OneFS?

Isilon's OneFS operating system is truly distributed and intelligently stripes data across all nodes in a cluster to create a single, shared pool of storage.
It combines the three layers of traditional storage architectures- file system, volume manager and RAID- into one unified software. It works by striping data across all nodes in a cluster and provide complete data availability with up to 4 node failures or 4 drive failures in a single node (n+4 data protection.)

Explain Consistency Groups?

I have seen application data often spans more than one volume.
So to manage operations spanning multiple volumes as a single group I create Consistency group. In a "consistency group" (CTG), all primary logical volumes are treated as a single entity.

Managing primary volumes as a consistency group allows replication and business continuity operations to be performed on all volumes in the group concurrently. Write order in secondary volumes is guaranteed across application logical volumes.

A Drive letter which is on a SAN LUN, doesn't come back after a reboot of Microsoft Windows Server? How to fix it?

I will CHKDSK.

It creates and displays a status report for a disk based on the file system. CHKDSK also lists and corrects errors on the disk.

A disk misses its drive letter when the drive's VSS attributes are changed to D (no default drive letter), H (hidden), and R (read only).

In that case:

I. Chkdsk against the drive with no switches results in chkdsk hanging at phase 0.

II. If chkdsk is run with /f switch then it returns that the disk is write protected.

I will use a utility called "vflag.exe" from Microsoft.

I will verify the state of the flags by using the vflag utility: vflag -display *

I will clear the incorrectly set flags using the vflag utility: vflag -clear X \\?\GLOBALROOT\Device\HarddiskVolumeN1N2

Where X is R for read only, D for no default drive letter, and H for hidden.

Name a Tier 1 Type Array?

Hitachi USPV

Fig: Hitachi USPV

Name a Tier 2 Type Array?

Hitachi AMS 2000 Midrange Storage Platform

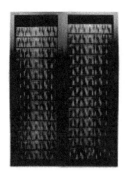

Fig: Hitachi AMS 2000 Midrange Storage Platform

Name a Tier 3 Type of Storage Array?

The HP Storage Works Modular SAN Array 1000 is an entry-level to mid-range Storage Area Network (SAN).

HP MSA1000 SAN storage

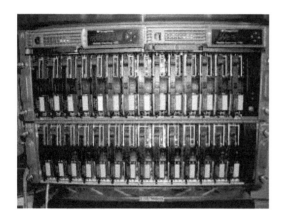

Fig: HP MSA1000 SAN storage

What is twisted Pair Cable?

A twisted pair cable has 2 independently insulated wires twisted around each other. This twisting of wires reduces electromagnetic interference and cross talk from neighboring wires.

Why Fibre optic cables are used?

Fibre optic cables have the following advantages over twisted pair cables:

I. Provide a greater bandwidth
II. May carry more data
III. Less susceptible to electromagnetic interference
IV. Allows data to be transmitted digitally

Is it possible to mix MultiMode 50 micon cables with MultiMode 62.5 micron cables?

Mixing MultiMode 50 micon cables with MultiMode 62.5 micron cables is supported but shortens the distances considerably because any place the 62.5 um goes into a 50 u cable there is a 4.5 dBm loss.

Explain how to calculate Buffer Credit?

The number of buffer credits that are required=(link speed in Gbps * distance in kilometers) / frame size in kilobytes

What switching components have you used storage network SAN?

I. Hub
II. Switch
III. Router
IV. Gigabit interface converter (GBIC)
V. Small form-factor pluggable (SFP)

Which File-Level Protocols you have used?

SMB, CIFS and NFS

What is the use of GBIC?

It converts digital signals to optical signals and optical signals to digital signals.

For sequential reads and writes, which RAID is good?

RAID-5

What is SAN Storage virtualization?

Physical storage resources are combined into storage pools, from which the logical storage is created.

What is thin provisioning?

Thin provisioning allows storage space to be allocated on an as needed basis.

What is a Dynamic Storage Pool?

It includes virtualization of internal and external heterogeneous storage into a single pool and benefits from the IOPs power of all spindles. I create the pools from multiple LDEVs from multiple array groups of any RAID level.

What SAN Storage Array supports Dynamic Storage Pool?

Hitachi Virtual Storage Platform VSP

Fig: Hitachi Virtual Storage Platform VSP

What SAN topologies exist?

5 Primary Types:

    I. Star
   II. Linear
  III. Circular
  IV. Tree
   V. Mesh

What is In-band?

In-band management access method to SAN involves managing devices through the common protocols such as telnet or SSH, using the network itself
Fibre Channel (fabric discovery) and storage management

What is Out-Of-Band?

Out-Of-Band Access method to a SAN will have an access server, that is connected to a management port of each controlled device. It Includes: IP network, serial port connected to terminal server, and SNMP using platform specific MIB.

What is a domain as it relates to a fabric?

Domain_ID is a unique numeric identifier for each switch in the fabric

What is FCID?

A switch assigns the FCID to each attached node, which is derived from the Domain_ID, Area_ID and WWN of the attached node.

What is principal switch?

Principal switch is responsible for distributing Name Server information throughout the fabric.

What is Core/Edge?

Fabric topology design where in storage ports are connected to "core" switches, which are in turn connected to edge switches (via ISL) which are connected to HBAs.

What type of switch you will use in the Edge tier?

Departmental switches

Examples: EMC Connectrix Switches

MDS-9148

Up to 48, 16-port base with 8-port increments 8 Gb/s FCP

MDS-9222i

Up to 70. Base includes 18 Fibre Channel and 4 IP ports.
Fig: EMC Connectrix Switch

What type of switch you will use in the Core?

Directors

For example: EMC Connectrix Directors

Model # ED-DCX-B

Fig: EMC Connectrix Directors

What applications and IOs have you worked with?

    I.   OLTP - Log Sequential
   II.   OLTP - Data Random
  III. Backup Sequential
  IV. Restore Sequential

Where should you keep log files?

RAID 1+0 since RAID 1+0 gives better write performance and availability than RAID 5.

What are the benefits of SAS?

    I.   SAS is full-duplex full bandwidth in both directions
   II.   Scalable I/O performance
  III. High reliability & redundancy
  IV. Point-to-point serial and simplified cabling
   V. Compatible with SATA & SAS HDDs & SSDs

SAS Roadmap:

     I. 6Gb/s SAS dual port, two streams
    II. 12Gb/s SAS dual port, two streams
  III. 12Gb/s SAS dual port, four streams
  IV. 12Gb/s MultiLink SAS™, four+ streams

Why RAID 5 not suitable for Data Base?

RAID 5 has a write penalty. DB is write-intensive.

What types of Read and write operations are going on in a SAN Array?

Read Hit, Read Miss, Fast Write and Delayed Fast Write

Can you calculate IOPS?

IOPS = 1/ [average latency (in sec) + average read/write seek time (in sec)]

Name long distance connectivity options?

    I. Coarse Wavelength Division Multiplexing
   II. Native FC over Dark Fibre
  III. Wave Division Multiplexing

How to find what kind of HBA is installed in AIX host?

lscfg –vp

How to find files in UNIX?

find . -name "nameoffile" -print

How will you scan for new disks which have been added to a tru64 host?

    I.   On Tru64 UNIX Version 4 # scu scan edit
   II. On Tru64 UNIX Version 5 # hwmgr scan scsi

How To check status of tape and take the tapes offline, in UNIX?

mt -f (drive path) status
mt -f (drive path) offline (To eject tape from drive)

Have you created LUNs?

Yes.

In EMC Symmetrix Storage I have used these commands to create LUNS

     symconfigure preview -file create_vols.cmd
     symconfigure prepare -file create_vols.cmd
     symconfigure commit -file create_vols.cmd

       where:

create_vols.cmd

```
create dev count=1, size= XXXX, emulation=fba,
        config=raid-5, disk_group=2;
```

Have you used a mechanism to discover Storage Array without requiring the in-band array connectivity to the host?

Yes. I have discovered EMC Symmetrix arrays using a remote SYMAPI server.

The symapisrv command controls the operation of the remote SYMAPI server, which provides a SYMCLI client/server connection

Explain your experience with infrastructure management software to monitor and analyze SANs. How to discover missing devices?

I have used ECC from EMC. ControlCenter improves storage utilization.

If the new Devices are missing in ECC I fix it by updating the database.

symcfg sync interrogates just the known Symmetrix units (previously discovered) that are accessible from the host, and updates the configuration and status information in the Symmetrix host database file. The information update can be confined to a specific Symmetrix unit.

```
symcfg discover
symcfg -sid 24 sync
```

```
symcfg LIST
or:
symcfg list
```

How you identify a Storage Array on SAN?

Before I begin to examine a storage configuration data, I try to identify it.

For example I have used Symmetrix Level Data to identify Symmetrix on SAN?

Each Symmetrix unit has a unique serial number called a Symmetrix ID
(SID). Using SYMCLI, you can get a list of all the accessible Symmetrix units
by SID, which also shows the model number and the number of
accessible devices in the unit. You can then choose a Symmetrix unit
from this list and get its configuration data. This high-level
information (such as the SID) is used with subsequent commands,
which can then lead you to configuration information for each of the
directors and devices within a unit.

List of Symmetrix

symcfg provides a list of Symmetrix IDs with one entry for each
Symmetrix unit accessible from the host.
For example, to get a list of Symmetrix units accessible from the host,
enter:
symcfg list

This command lists what Symmetrix configuration is current in your
host database. To update the database, run symcfg sync.

Have you used Locks in Storage Arrays? Examples?

Yes.

Lock is a security feature that restricts host access to storage arrays.

For example EMC Symmetrix uses various locks for it SAN operations.

It uses SID (source ID) lock a security feature that restricts host access to Symmetrix storage
arrays by adding switch source ID information to the VCM database.

SID prevents WWN spoofing when multiple hosts are connected to the same storage port.

To query for external device locks, issue:

symdev -lock list

> To manually release the lock, issue:
> symdev -lock # release.
> symcfg -lock list

> Some examples of Locks I have seen on Symmetrix:

A. Lock 0
   General lock used to lock the entire symmetrix. Used with srdf controls on both the local and remote symmetrix

B. Lock 12
   Lock used by application registration feature (run symcfg list -app -v).

C. Lock 13
   Old version optimizer locks for updating the optimizer mailbox (symoptmz)

D. Lock 15
   Configuration lock - taken by "symconfigure", sddr, even though sddr is not an api user, and optimizer.

Symmetrix External Locks

Symmetrix external locks are used by SYMAPI (locks 0 to 15) and also
for applications assigned by EMC (>15) to lock access to the entire
Symmetrix during critical operations. (SRDF operations use lock 0
and the Optimizer uses lock 13.)
If you need to see what Symmetrix units (local and remote) have a
Symmetrix external lock number 0, enter:
symcfg -lock list
To release an external lock 0 (hang) on a Symmetrix unit, enter:
symcfg -sid 0XYZ98712341357 -lockn 0 release

How you View Application Registrations on an Array?

On a Symmetrix Array I have used symcfg.

You can view all the applications (registered in a Symmetrix) that
have accessed a certain Symmetrix, to which your host is connected.
For example, to list all the applications that are have worked with
Symmetrix 043303, enter:
symcfg list -applications -sid 043303
Viewing Hosts with

Symmetrix Access
You can view all the hosts that have accessed a certain Symmetrix units), to which your host is connected.

Explain your experience with managing the Devices on an Array by Commands?

I have used symcli commands to manage Symmetrix:
For example, to list all the host names on a Symmetrix 043303, enter:
symcfg list -connections -sid 043303
In the example above, the display of the host connections are organized according to each Symmetrix.
You can view all the hosts, sorted by host names first and then the Symmetrix connections second.
For example, to list all the host connections, sorted by host names that have worked with visible Symmetrix units, enter:
symcfg list -connections –sorthost

symcfg list -address -fa -available all   lists all fibre directors in a symmetrix system and which devices they can access

How to view Storage Capacities to Hosts?

You can view the storage capacities of all the hosts that have accessed a certain Symmetrix, to which your host is connected.
For example, to list the allocated storage capacities of all the host names that have worked with Symmetrix 043303, enter:
symcfg list -connections -capacity -sid 043303

How will you be verifying Network Services?

You can view the available network services in the client/SYMAPI Server connection.
For example, to list the network services in your connection, enter:
symcfg list –services

You found that you have a problem with one director. How you can check the config?

Use symcfg to get configuration and status information about all the directors in the Symmetrix unit.
For example, to get information about all the directors, enter:
symcfg -dir all list
This command provides information such as:
The director ID
The Symmetrix slot number in which the director resides
The type of the director
The status of the director
You can get configuration and status information about one or all directors of a certain type. For example, to get information about all the front-end directors (SA and FA), enter:
symcfg -sa all list
This command provides information such as:
The director ID
The Symmetrix slot number in which the director resides
The type of the director
The status of the director
You can view the port status information to see if the ports are online or offline on SA or FA directors. For example, to get the port status on all SA and FA directors, enter:
symcfg -sa all list –port

What products you have used to create duplication within a disk array?

ShadowImage and SnapShot both create duplication within a disk array.

ShadowImage: When a hardware failure occurs in the P-VOL, it has no effect on the S-VOL.

SnapShot: Amount of physical data to be used for the V-VOL is small because only the differential data is managed.

Explain your experience with a snapshot provider and Windows Server and Dynamic Disk?

I have used Hitachi HDS *SHADOW IMAGE* a hardware-based snapshot provider. In an environment of the Windows Server 2000/Windows Server, I cannot use Shadow Image pair volumes as dynamic disk because S-VOL is displayed as Foreign in Disk Management and become inaccessible after re-synchronizing.

You got replication Link error? How you can check?

For a SRDF Link error:

RA can be offline and Online to Reset.
Taking RA Directors Offline
You can take RDF director(s) of a specified Symmetrix offline.
For example, to take RA-12 of Symmetrix 043033 offline, enter:
symcfg offline -RA 12 -sid 123
To bring the director back online, enter:
symcfg online -RA 12 -sid 123

Taking Front-End Director Ports Offline:

You can take a certain port of a front-end director offline.
For example, to take port 1 of SA-12 in Symmetrix 043033 offline, enter:
symcfg offline -SA 12 -P 1 -sid 123

Note: If you turn off the only connection from your host to your Symmetrix, you will not be able to contact the Symmetrix in order to turn it back on (online).

Using another host, to bring the director port back online, enter:
symcfg online -SA 12 -P 1 -sid 123

Explain WAFL: Write Anywhere File Layout?

I. WAFL (Write Anywhere File Layout) is a high-performance journaling file system used in Network Appliance's NAS and caching devices.

II. It natively supports RAID implementations and allows for expansion on the fly.
III. A RAID 4 uses block-level striping with a dedicated parity disk. This allows each member of the set to act independently when only a single block is requested.
IV. It does it by a system of pointers to disk clusters that take up a small amount of extra disk space, WAFL enables up to 31 snapshots of the disk to be scheduled in order to roll back to previous versions of the data.

V. By storing system metadata (inodes, block maps, and inode maps) in the same way application data is stored, WAFL is able to write file system metadata blocks anywhere on the disk.

How Device Level Data is maintained?

The Symmetrix database file maintains device level or low level configuration and status information for each device on every Symmetrix unit that is accessible from the host.
Using SYMCLI, you can get a list of all the available devices. You can then choose a device from this list and get its configuration and status information. This information can lead you to back-end information for the device's disk director(s) and corresponding hyper-volumes, and their mapping to disk drives.

Tell us a generic method for SAN based replication?

I. I will select a volume on the production array that needs to be replicated
II. I will create a volume on the remote array that will contain the copy
III. I will establish a Fibre Channel or iSCSI link between the local and remote arrays
IV. I will make the initial copy across the link on the remote array. The array performs the subsequent processing independently from I/O processing.

How will you setup & modify RDF attribute from a device?

convert dev SymDevName to DeviceConfig;

    I.   RDF1   : convert dev X to Unprotected
   II.   RDF1+Mir   : convert dev X to 2-Way-Mir
  III. RDF1+R-S   : convert dev X to RAID-S
  IV. RDF1+R-5   : convert dev X to RAID-5
   V. RDF1-BCV   : convert dev X to BCV
  VI. RDF1-BCV-Mir : convert dev X to 2-Way-BCV-Mir
 VII. RDF1-BCV+R-5 : convert dev X to BCV+R-5

How can you get all the devices listed?

sympd and symdev

Use sympd to get a list that shows all physical device (pd) names (in the left column) with the corresponding Symmetrix device (dev) names (in the next column) for all devices (visible to your host) on a Symmetrix unit.
For example, to get a list of physical device names, enter:
sympd list
Use symdev to list all Symmetrix device (dev) names for all devices on a Symmetrix unit.
For example, to get a list of Symmetrix device names, enter:
symdev list

How you can find new devices?

By rebuilding the database.

If you reconfigured your Symmetrix by adding or removing devices seen by the host since the last time you updated the database, you need to use symcfg discover. This command causes the host to rescan all SCSI buses and to rebuild the database with information about all the discovered and accessible devices.
If you physically disconnected a Symmetrix unit from the host system, the data for this Symmetrix remains in the database. Since the Symmetrix is physically disconnected from the host, no new information can be returned with which to update the database. If the

disconnection is permanent, you should run symcfg remove. If you are uncertain about whether a Symmetrix is still connected, run syminq.

Replication is failing. What you can do?

For SRDF:

Device External Locks SYMAPI uses device external locks in the Symmetrix to lock BCV pairs during Time Finder and RDF pairs during SRDF control operations. To list a range of Symmetrix devices (0000 to 000A) that have a device external lock, enter:
symdev list -sid 870 -RANGE 0000:000A -lock
On your host, if you discover a lock that has been on for well over 2 hours and are sure no one is using the device resources, you can choose to release the lock. To release the device lock on a range of Symmetrix devices in Symmetrix 870, enter:
symdev release -sid 870 -RANGE 0000:000A

Explain some replication Component Commands?

For SRDF:

The SRDF commands allow you to perform control operations on RDF devices.

The symrdf command also performs operations including:

Setting the RDF mode for one or more RDF pairs in a device group
Returning information about the state of RDF mirroring
Ping one or more Symmetrix units locally or remotely via SRDF links
Singular SRDF control operations, which are the individual operations that comprise the composite SRDF control actions

symrdf

Performs the following control operations on RDF devices:

I. Establishes (mirror) an RDF pair by initiating a data copy from the source (R1) side to the target (R2) side. This operation can be a full or incremental establish.

I. Restores remote mirroring. Initiates a data copy from the target (R2) side to the source (R1) side. This operation can be a full or incremental restore.

II. Splits an RDF pair, which stops mirroring for the RDF pair(s) in a device group.
Failover from the source (R1) side to the target (R2) side, switching data processing to the target (R2) side.

III. Failback from the target (R2) side to the source (R1) side, switching data processing to the source (R1) side.

IV. Updates the source (R1) side after a failover, while the target (R2) side may still be operational to its local host(s).

V. Swaps the source (R1) and target (R2) destinations between the target and the source.

VI. Establishes or deletes Dynamic SRDF device pairs.

symreplicate

Invokes a replicate session that generates automated recurrent, background copies of the standard data following a path across SRDF links and cascading BCVs.
You can start a replicate session,
stop it, and restart the replicate session.

Explain replication operation?

For SRDF operation:

The Symmetrix Remote Data Facility (SRDF) is a business continuance solution that maintains a mirror image of data at the device level in Symmetrix systems located in physically separate sites.
SRDF provides a recovery solution for component or site failures between remotely mirrored devices. SRDF reduces backup and recovery costs and significantly reduces recovery time after a disaster.
In an SRDF configuration, the individual Symmetrix devices are designated as either a source or a target to synchronize and coordinate SRDF activity.
If the source (R1) device fails, the data on its corresponding target (R2) device can be accessed. When the source (R1) device is replaced, the source (R1) device can be resynchronized.
SRDF configurations have at least one source (R1) device mirrored to

one target (R2) device.

Explain some troubleshooting you can do for replication issues?

In EMC storage array-*BASED REPLICATION* product *SRDF:*

Query SRDF Devices after executing any SRDF control operation, use the symrdf query command to verify the results and impact on selected devices and device groups.

The symrdf query argument can be used with the -g DgName, -cg CgName and -file FileName options.

To view the SRDF details about all devices in device group prod,
enter:
symrdf -g prod query

The query results provide details about each RDF pair in the device group, including:

Logical device name
Physical device name
Number of invalid tracks on R1 and R2
SRDF link state
RDF modes
RDF local and remote SRDF states
RDF pair state

Ping SRDF Devices You can use the symrdf -rdf ping option to determine if a Symmetrix unit that is connected via SRDF links is up and running.
The Symmetrix units are pinged via the SRDF links. Based on return codes, you can determine whether some or all of the Symmetrix units were successfully pinged.

For example, to ping Symmetrix unit 123 via the SRDF links, enter:
symrdf -rdf -sid 123 ping

Verify SRDF States You can verify that the RDF pairs are in the Synchronized or Restored states.

For example, to verify that the RDF pair DEV007, in device group
prod, is in the Synchronized state, enter:
symrdf -g prod verify DEV007

Explain Control Operations in a replication?

For EMC SRDF:

SRDF control operations, which are performed with the symrdf
command, support the high level operations of the SRDF
environment, such as failover (disaster recovery), backup or copy
(decision support), and concurrent operations.

How can you create a remote synchronous copy of production file systems at a remote location in NAS?

On a Celerra NAS :
By using Celera SRDF

Name a multi pathing software?

PowerPath is server-resident software that enhances application availability by providing
automatic path failover and recovery functionality. EMC® PowerPath® software is a server-
resident, performance and application availability enhancing software solution. PowerPath
combines multiple path I/O capabilities, automatic load balancing, and path failover
functions into one integrated package.

Have you managed multipathing via command line?

Yes. I have used Power path command CLI:

PowerPath Path Management Commands

powermt Command
    I.   powermt Manage a PowerPath® environment.
    II. powercf Configure PowerPath devices (Solaris only).

III. emcpreg Manage PowerPath license registration.
IV. emcpminor Check for free minor numbers.
V. emcpupgrade Convert PowerPath configuration files.
VI. emcpadm List available PowerPath pseudo device names, list used PowerPath
VII. pseudo device names, or rename PowerPath pseudo device (Solaris
VIII. and Linux only).
IX. emcphostid Set or reset the host ID (HP-UX 11i v2.0 and higher and Linux only).
X. powervxvm Places PowerPath pseudo devices under Veritas Volume Manager control (Solaris and AIX only). Needed only with VxVM 4.0 and earlier. Command Description
XI. powermt check Check for, and optionally remove, dead paths.
XII. Powermt check_registration   Check the state of the PowerPath license.
XIII. powermt config Configure logical devices as PowerPath devices.
XIV. powermt display
XV. powermt watch
XVI. Display the state of HBAs configured for
XVII. PowerPath. powermt watch is deprecated.
XVIII. powermt display options Display options settings for storage system classes.
XIX. powermt remove Remove a path from the PowerPath configuration.
XX. powermt restore Test and restore paths.
XXI. powermt save Save a custom PowerPath configuration.
XXII. powermt set mode Set paths to active or standby mode.
XXIII. powermt set
XXIV. periodic_autorestore

Enable or disable periodic autorestore
XXV. powermt set policy Change the load balancing and failover policy.
XXVI. powermt set priority Set the I/O priority.

In a HDS Hitachi SAN how will you perform path failover, fail back, and automatic load balancing?

I. Hitachi Dynamic Link Manager Software
II. dlnkmgr view

How to monitor and manage all replication systems in HDS SAN? How to verify Recovery Point Objective (RPO)?

Hitachi Replication Manager

How will you manage (Create Pool, Lun & Map) Hitachi storage systems?

Device Manger

Explain iSCSI naming conventions?

iSCSI has two schemes for naming nodes (initiators or targets
iqn (iSCSI qualified name) – Based on reverse Domain Name System (DNS)
eui (extended unique identifier) – Same as FC World-Wide Names.

Name a product that can create a point in time snapshot?

Celerra SnapSure:

Snap Sure is a software feature for Celerra that creates a point-in-time snapshot of the filesystem.

Explain different methods of flushing in write cache?

 I. Idle flushing
 II. Watermark flushing

III.   Forced flushing

You Presented SAN Storage on a HP-UX, How will you discover?

On an HP UNIX server, after provisioning storage from Symmetrix:

Discover

    I. symcfg discover
    II. symmask refresh
    III. symcfg discover

Build New Devices:
    I.   ioscan
    II.   insf
    III. symcfg discover
    IV. inq | syminq

PowerPath:
    I.   powermt restore
    II.   powermt check
    III. powermt config
    IV. powermt save

Name the component in Storage Array which is used to present device to host?

In a symmetric Array:

A Channel director

Define a replication product?

SRDF

SRDF provides comprehensive business continuity and restart capabilities for both planned and unplanned outages. This online, host-independent, mirrored data solution, duplicates production site data on one or more physically separate target Symmetrix systems. Systems can be across the room, across the globe, or anywhere in between.

For which component failure in DMX, Port Bypass card is used?

Disk director

How will you add a SAN Storage based disk tape library to Solaris OS?

    I.   I will check to make sure Solaris host's /dev/rmt directory has no virtual libraries and no devices.
   II.   Then I will create virtual library and enable access to the server.
  III.   rem_drv st to remove the entries in the /dev/rmt directory/ rm *.
  IV.   add_drv st to create the /dev/rmt device files.
   V.   devfsadm to create the device links.
  VI.   mt -f /dev/rmt/0 status.
 VII.   Reconfigure reboot the server (-- -r)
VIII.   Modify the st.conf file as in the following example:

```
name="st" parent="fp" target=0;
name="st" class="scsi" target=0 lun=0;
```

In a SAN with EMC storage how will you check if there is a bad disk?

symdisk list -hypers -v -sid xxxx

Bad drives will show up as "Not Ready".

How many mirrors are possible with STD device?

BCV mirror

2

Which protocol is used in windows to share file?

Common Internet File System (CIFS)

It requires:
    I.   Authentication,
   II.   Mapping and
  III.   Authorization

How data is handled in a backup copy mirror establish?

The *TIMEFINDER* family of software provides trusted local storage replication leveraging the high-end Symmetrix VMAX Architecture.

In time finder mirror establish

Copy from STD device to BCV

Name the replication operation in which link is suspended between R1 and R2, Read and write enable on R1 , R2

In SRDF Operation:

Split

What are the operations you have for the mode of data mover fail over?

Auto, Retry, Manual

How will you Ensure Fibre Channel Security?

I. Physical security: Badge Aceess to Data Center
II. Lock Down E_port creation
III. Disable ports
IV. Data encryption: I can use datafort. A DataFort is positioned between the backup servers on the SAN and the TAN, acting as the encryption agent and stores data encrypted when needed.
V. Zoning & LUN masking

How to troubleshoot SCSI Bus Resets?

ANSI SCSI standard provides a method called BUS RESET to force the bus and its devices into a known state.

A host typically asserts a RESET signal one or more times on each of its SCSI buses when it first starts up and when it shuts down.

This reset is initiated by the SCSI Driver for the HBA and usually follows a specific sequence:

A. HARD reset the target device first (tape or disk).

B. HARD reset all of the devices on the BUS

C. HARD reset the HBA or SCSI controller itself.

I have seen this due to outdated firmware on the HBA\devices and bad cables.

How will you synchronize system times on multiple UNIX servers?

I will use rdate command.

rdate - set system date from a remote host

SYNOPSIS
    rdate hostname

DESCRIPTION
    rdate sets the local date and time from the hostname given as an argu-ment.

What Types of Configuration are possible with Replications?

I can answer this with regard to SRDF:

SRDF offers three types of configuration: Uni-directional, Bi-directional, and Dual Configuration.

   I.   Uni-directional is a one way mirror relationship.
   II. Bi-directional is a two-way mirror relationship.
   III. Dual Configuration is two uni-directional configurations.

What Replication Modes you familiar with?

SRDF Modes
Five operational modes are possible on SRDF logical Volumes:

   I.   Synchronous mode,
   II.   Semi-Synchronous mode,
   III. Adaptive Copy-Write Pending mode,
   IV.   Adaptive Copy-Disk,
   V.   Copy mode; and
   VI.   Domino.

These operational modes only affect those Symmetrix volumes that are remotely mirrored. I/O operations with local volumes occur as if they are in a non-SRDF environment as no updates are required to volumes at a different physical location.

There is a preferred mode of operation for each SRDF solution.
These operational modes are selectable based on requirements of performance, distance, and speed of recovery.

If data cannot be copied from the R1 to the R2 when consistency protection is enabled, what will happen?

For SRDF/A:

All devices in the group will be made not ready on the link to preserve R2 data consistency.

Which hard drives currently you have used in your SAN?

I. Flash drives for Extreme performance and Lowest Latency

II. Serial Attached SCSI (SAS)   with 10 and 15k rpm because it's Cost Effective and provides Better performance

III. NL-SAS drives with   7200 rpm, it has Performance and reliability that is equivalent to SATA drives

Explain why a LUN is trespassed in a Array?

How to restore it?

When there is a failure in the primary I/O path, a LUN is trespassed to maintain access to the data using an alternate path.

In Clariion Storage Array:

Restoring the SP returns all LUNs to their default owner.

What is the difference between Fan-Out and Fan-in?

Fan-Out: Ratio of Storage Ports to Hosts
Fan-In: Ratio of Hosts to Storage Ports

Which platform you suggest for virtual applications with VMware and Hyper-V integration?

How to add one system to another?

EMC VNX Series: High-performing unified storage

To add one VNX system to another

I will use Unisphere as:

All Systems > Domains > Local Domain > Add/Remove Systems

You are unable to upgrade firmware on a SAN switch, what could be a reason?

On a Brocade switch:

The Alarm setting on Brocade switch causes the firmware download to fail.

The Alarm settings must be removed by:

GUI Web Tools > Fabric Watch > Fabric.

Why should you upgrade Firmware and Drivers of HBA's?

Firmware is the software that runs ON the device. It provides intelligence to the device.
A driver is the software that communicates with the operating system.

The driver and the firmware for a particular FC HBA must interact with each other to provide proper error handling and throttling within a SAN.
Any variations in newer or older versions of firmware or the driver can cause problems and communication issues between these components.

With every new releases of firmware a new functionality is added. So an upgrade of a firmware to the latest version can cause problems with the older driver.

Give an example of random I/O workloads?

Microsoft Exchange and SQL Server

Which HDD you have used in a Storage Array?

Type	Bus Speed	Distance	Cable Pins

I.	FC	400MB/s	10K m	4
II.	SATA-II	300MB/s	6 m	22
III.	SAS	300MB/s	10 m	22

For optimal performance of a LUN accessed by Windows hosts what you suggest?

I will configure disk partitions to begin on sector boundaries that are divisible by 64K matching the RAID stripe segment size.

I can use Diskpart to convert a basic disk to a dynamic disk and also to verify alignment:

DISKPART> list partition

How will you keep track of invalid tracks in replication?

For Time Finder and SRDF:

I will use Deltamark also called Change Tracker, which is the symchg command in Solutions Enabler.

SYNOPSIS

symchg [-sid SymmID] [-v] [-h]

Which enterprise SAN arrays you have used?

I. EMC VMAX Family, VNX Family, Isilon, Atmos, Xtreme Family, VSPEX
II. Fujitsu Eternus DX8700 S3/DX8900 S3 CD10000 hyperscale storage
III. Hitachi Data Systems (HDS) Virtual Storage Platform (VSP) G1000
IV. Hewlett-Packard (HP) XP7 Storage system HP 3PAR StoreServ 20000
V. IBM System Storage DS8000 IBM Flash System V9000
VI. NetApp All-Flash FAS, FAS Storage Systems, FAS8000 Series

Which RAIDs you have used? Explain its specifications?

1) Raid 0 (Stripe):
    (1) Minimum 2 disks.
    (2) No redundancy
    (3) It offers a much improved I/O performance when reading and writing data.

2) Raid 1 (Mirror):
    (1) 2 Drives
    (2) High performance
    (3) High redundancy
    (4) When a block of data is written, write process is exactly duplicated on another disk.

3) Raid 5 (Drives with Parity):
    (1) Minimum 3 Drives
    (2) Good performance
    (3) Good redundancy
    (4) Good Price
    (5) A single read requires the whole stripe to be read.

4) Raid 6 (Drives with Double Parity):
    (1) Minimum 4 Drives
    (2) Extension of RAID 5 that allows for additional fault tolerance
    (3) RAID 6 does not have a performance penalty for read operations, but it does have a performance penalty on write.
    (4) RAID-6 is best used for workloads that are mostly read, or highly sequential. Because of the 2 parity calculations there is a higher Read/Write/Modify penalty for RAID-6 than RAID-5.
    RAID-6 is not recommended for random write workloads.

5) Raid 10 (Mirror+Stripe) or 0+1 (Stripe+Mirror):
    (1) Minimum 4 Drives
    (2) Stripe of mirrors
    (3) Excellent redundancy
    (4) Excellent performance
    (5) Usable capacity 50% of available disk drives

6) Raid 50 (Parity+Stripe):
    (1) Minimum 6 Drives
    (2) Usable capacity is between 67% - 94%

7) Raid 60 (Double Parity+Stripe):

(1) Minimum 8 Drives
(2) Usable capacity 50% - 88%

Why Writes on RAID are different?

RAID level has different write penalty:
For example RAID-1would require 2 x Writes and 1 x Read, because the write operation is mirrored and hence RAID 1 Write penalty is 2.
Accordingly:

RAID Level	IO Penalty
B. RAID 0	1
C. RAID 1	2
D. RAID 5	4
E. RAID 6	6
F. RAID 10	2

How will you analyze network packets from NAS?

I can use these tools:

I. Snoop

snoop - capture and inspect network packets

SYNOPSIS
    snoop [-aqrCDINPSvV] [-t [r | a | d]] [-c maxcount]
        [-d device] [-i filename] [-n filename] [-o filename]
        [-p first [, last]] [-s snaplen] [-x offset [, length]]
        [expression]

II. Ethereal

ethereal   - Interactively   browse network traffic

SYNOPSYS

    ethereal   [-a capture autostop condition   ] ...
    [-b number of ring buffer files   ] [-B byte view height   ]
    [-c count] [-f capture filter expression] [-h]
    [-i interface]   [-k] [-l] [-m font] [-n]
    [-N resolving flags] [-o preference setting] ...

[-p] [-P packet list height]   [-Q] [-r infile]
[-R display filter expression]   [-S] [-s snaplen]
[-T tree view height] [-t time stamp format] [-v]
[-w savefile] [-z statistics-string] [infile   ]

DESCRIPTION

Ethereal   is a GUI network protocol analyzer.

III. tcpdump

tcpdump - dump traffic on a network

Synopsis
tcpdump [-AdDefIKlLnNOpqRStuUvxX] [-B buffer_size] [-c count]
[-C file_size] [-G rotate_seconds] [-F file]
[-i interface] [-m module] [-M secret]
[-r file] [-s snaplen] [-T type] [-w file]
[-W filecount]
[-E]
[-y datalinktype] [-z postrotate-command] [-Z user] [expression]
Description
Tcpdump prints out a description of the contents of packets on a network interface that
match the boolean expression

Why it's difficult to backup a replicated file system?

How can you backup a replicated file system?

During replication sync on the target the SavVol are locked for a File System.

An integrated NDMP Checkpoint can be used with SnapSure enabled in the Backup
application.

You need a Large LUN but you can not create metaLUNs, what can you do?

I will use Logical volume manager to create and manage the storage of servers.

Linux File System Management:

Linux LVM to create a large 3TB partition size.

Parted is a GNU utility, which is used to manipulate the hard disk partition.
To create a partition start GNU parted as follows:

   I. # parted /dev/sdb
  II. (parted) mklabel gpt
 III. (parted) mkpart primary 0 3T
 IV. (parted) quit
  V. pvcreate initializes Physical Volume for later use by the Logical Volume Manager
 VI. # pvcreate /dev/sdb1
 VII. vgcreate creates a new volume group:
VIII. # vgcreate myvolume /dev/sdb1
 IX. lvcreate creates a new logical volume in a volume group
  X. # lvcreate -L 3TB myvolume
 XI. mkfs utility is used to create filesystem
 XII. mkfs -t ext3 -m 1 -v
XIII. # mkfs.ext3 /dev/mapper/myvolume-lvol0

Explain the use of fsck (File System Check) on SAN storage? What are fsck various phases?

fsck (file system consistency check) is a command used to check filesystem for consistency errors and repair them on Linux/UNIX filesystems.

FSCK errors are usually caused by a busy file system, system crash.

Here are its phases:

pass0 - checking structural files
pass1 - checking inode sanity and blocks
pass2 - checking directory linkage
pass3 - checking reference counts
pass4 - checking resource maps

In your SAN report you see high "ENC out" errors, why?

Enc out errors are created by hardware fault, cable, SFP, HBA

How to display speed of SAN switch port?

For Brocade switch port:

A. To see the port speed: portcfgshow

B. To change speed of port: portcfgspeed

Explain the difference between Full duplex and Half duplex?

I. Full-duplex data transmission means that data can be transmitted in both directions on a signal carrier at the same time.

II. A half-duplex (HDX) system provides communication in both directions, but only one direction at a time

Which Seven Tiers of Disaster Recovery was originally defined by SHARE to help identify the various methods of recovering mission-critical computer systems as required supporting business continuity?

Tier 0: No off-site data – Possibly no recovery
Tier 1: Data backup with no hot site
Tier 2: Data backup with a hot site
Tier 3: Electronic vaulting
Tier 4: Point-in-time copies
Tier 5: Transaction integrity
Tier 6: Zero or near-Zero data loss
Tier 7: Highly automated, business integrated solution

After a firmware load on a SAN switch a port where an AIX host is connected is showing not ready, how to fix it?

      I.   I will enable the port

     II.   I will run Configuration Manager (cfgmgr)

Does NDMP support file level deduplication?

No.

NDMP can back up the compressed version of the file.

How to view free space of disks in a Storage Array that are mapped to DA (disk) directors?

On a Symmetrix array:

symdev list -sid xxx -da all -space

How will you find the volumes which are not mapped to a front end channel on the Storage Array?

On a Symmetrix Array I can do this by:

symdev list -no port

How to find a failed disk on a Storage Array?

I have used this command on a Symmetrix Array to find a failed disk:
symdisk -sid xxx list -failed

Which parameter will tell you if a write operation could be sent directly to cache?

% Hit

Which performance indicator shows information about Writes pending?

I. System Max WP limit: The percent of the target % at which writes are delayed. The range is from 40% to 80%.

II. % Cache WP: Percent of system cache that is write pending

You provisioned SAN Storage to an AIX host, which filesystem you recommend if the user needs a 10TB filesystem?

JFS2: Enhanced Journaled File System.
The recommended maximum size for a JFS2 is 16 TB.
JFS2 is designed to accommodate a 64-bit kernel and larger files.

How will you make sure that AIX host is capable of running JFS2?

JFS2 can run on the 64-bit kernel.
I can verify that by:
/usr/sbin/bootinfo -K
returns "32" if the 32-bit kernel is enabled and "64" if the 64-bit kernel is enabled.

Have you used ODM in AIX?

ODM is a database of system and device configuration information integrated into the OS. It is intended for storing system information.

 ODM parts:

 I. Object Classes: Are database files, where each file is called an object class.
 II. Objects: Each object class consists of objects.
 III. Descriptors: Describe the layout of the objects.

Storage vendors provide ODM definitions for their AIX customers and here are some commands I have used:

To display object class definition: odmshow
To retrive objects from an Object Class: odmget
To delete objects: odmdelete

Users of NAS device are complaining that NAS is very slow to transfer files, what can you check?

It can happen if FC target ports unequally loaded.

I will rebalance the path by selecting automatic selection algorithm.

You have Continuous Data Replication but there is a need to change the data on destination. Is it possible?

Data on the destination should never be changed. If that happens it will be considered inconsistent and Full Re-Sync will be required for rebuilding it.

You are using multipathing. What parameter you enable for path health checking?

I. Auto Failback

II. Path Health Checking

Explain the use of SCSI Reservation?

Have you seen a negative consequence of SPC-2 SCSI?

A SCSI Reserve/Reservation is put on a LUN by a host OS to prevent other hosts or applications from gaining unauthorized access. The SCSI reserve is a bit set in Shared Memory.

The negative consequence of SPC-2 SCSI reserve occurs if the HBA that owns the reservation fails. The reservation must be broken.

To break negative reservation,

I. SCSI reset

II. Bus device reset

III. LUN device reset

IV. Power cycle

V. Fibre Channel link reset

How will you add a new Fibre switch to an active zone set?

On New switch:

I. Disable the switch: [switchdisable]

II. Clear the config: [cfgclear & cfgsave]

III. Change the domain ID : Unique Domain ID

IV. ISL : Configure two ports as E ports : [portcfgeport]

V. Disable those two ports [portdisable]

On existing switch:

I. Free two ports for ISL

II. Disable those two ports: [portdisable]

III. Physically connect cables across switches.

IV. Enable those ports on both switches one after other

V. Distribute Zone set by enabling a Full Zone Set Distribution

Explain Zoning Structure?

Zone Set ⇔ Zones ⇔ Zone Members ⇔ Zone Alias Members ⇔ Zone Alias

What is the difference between Fiber Channel Nodes and ports?

I. A node port (N_Port) is a port on a network node
II. Nodes can be Hosts or Devices, such as a servers or storage device
III. The ports are the bus adapters

How Nodes communicate?

Nodes communicate via three topologies

I. Point to point
II. Loop
III. Fabric

A file system from NAS was exported to a Linux server but you can not NFS mount it. What can you do?

portmap provides coordination between RPC services and the port numbers used to communicate with them:

I will start this service by:

#chkconfig portmap on

#service portmap start

Then I will start the NFS file system:

service nfs start

The NFS server is the machine which makes file systems available to the network. It does so by either exporting or sharing them.

What is the difference between hard and soft mount?

SOFT MOUNTS:

It will fail after a few retries if a remote partition becomes unavailable.
Soft mounts should only be used if we are only reading from a disk,.
This mount is an unreliable one.

HARD MOUNTS:

They are permanent mounts designed to look just like any normal, local file system. If a partition that is hard mounted becomes unavailable, client programs will keep trying to access it forever. This will cause local processes to lock when a hard mounted disk goes away. Hard mounts are the default type of mount.

You have setup NAS and you want to find out which clients have mounted NFS exports?

showmount -e server-Ip-address of NFS server

showmount - show mount information for an NFS server

SYNOPSIS
/usr/sbin/showmount   [-adehv]   [--all]   [--directories]
[--exports] [--help] [--version] [host]

DESCRIPTION
showmount queries the mount daemon on a remote host for information
about the state of the NFS server on that machine.

Have you used devices to communicate with Storage Array?

Yes. I have used Gatekeeper devices in EMC Storage array.

Gatekeeper devices are Symmetrix devices that act as the target of command requests to
Enginuity based functionality. They are used to facilitate the special communication that
controls the Symmetrix array.

How will you bring a replication adapter online?

I have brought RA adapter online. It has hardware and software switch.

I will enable the Hardware switch of the director within the Symmetrix and then I will
enable its software switch:

symcfg -sid xx -RA xx online

How will you Write-disable the local device in a replication?

I will Write-disable the local devices: R1 devices as:

symrdf -g <groupname> write_disable r1 -force

How will you calculate correct number of Replication adapters?

While setting up EMC SRDF I had calculated Remote Adapters (RA) using formula:

N+1 RAs, where N is the number of RAs required.
It will provide redundancy. It will allow standby adapter to become the active one temporarily, until the original can be restored and brought back online.

What will you monitor in replication?

In replication writes are from cache to cache, Frequency of Read write requests, the amount of data coming into the array.
I will monitor:
  I. Cycle
  II. Requests
  III. Cache

How can you verify the size of a veritas file system on UNIX?

mkfs -F vxfs

Which filesystem supports NFS4 ACL's and how to create it?

Only JFS2 with extended attribute Version 2 (J2) supports NFS V4 ACLs.

To create a JFS2 file system:
mkfs -V jfs2

In a SAN environment with replication when physical links goes offline and soon comes back online what will happen?

I have seen that If physical link goes down and comes up, the replication adapter stays hung. For example in a SAN environment with EMC Symmetrix Remote Data Facility I had to reset RA to get the link backup as:

symcfg -RA 6a -sid xyz offline
symcfg -RA 6a -sid xyz online

On AIX you have attached a LUN which is greater than 1TB, but you see many SC & SENSE Data errors on the host? Why?

Lun/Dev is greater than 1 TB is not supported on a 32 bit kernel.

bootinfo -k will tell me if it's a 32 bit kernel.
I will Convert the kernel to 64 bit as:
    I. ln -sf /usr/lib/boot/unix_64 /unix
  II. ln -sf /usr/lib/boot/unix_64 /usr/lib/ boot/unix

III. Use the BOSBOOT command to re-create the boot image :
bosboot -ad /dev/ipldevice
IV. shutdown –Fr
V. bootinfo -K will now show me 64 bit

Have you used Kernel-based Virtual Machine?

Kernel-based Virtual Machine (KVM) is a virtualization infrastructure for the Linux kernel. KVM requires a processor with hardware virtualization extension.
Using KVM, I can run multiple virtual machines running unmodified Linux or Windows images.

How will you improve disk I/O performance on a SAN connected LINUX Server?

I will tune the The bdflush parameters.
This file /proc/sys/vm/bdflush controls the operation of the bdflush kernel daemon.
It is related to the operation of the virtual memory.
I generally tune this file to improve file system performance.
I make it wait little more write to disk and thus avoid some disk access contention.

How will you unmount busy devices on UNIX?

To kill process that is keeping filesystem busy

fuser -k /mountpoint

How to List files in UNIX?

cd - change directory

ls - list contents of current directory
ls -a - all files
ls -F - show types
ls -l - show long listing, including access permissions

Have you worked as a SAN Administrator? What were your responsibilities?

Yes.

Responsibilities:

Administration and Maintenance

Day-to-day implementation and configuration of systems within the SAN, Fibre channel host bus adapter and drivers management, LUN Masking, Fibre Channel Switch Administration
Software upgrades & trouble shooting

Switch Fabric Administration

Software upgrades
Firmware upgrades
License Management
Backup Switch Configuration

Storage Frame Administration

Software upgrades
Firmware upgrades
License Management
Storage Reconfiguration

Tell us most important commands, CLI to manage a Brocade SAN?

I refer to Brocade Fabric OS Command Reference from Brocade and use these commands, command line interface to manage SAN switches

I. aliRemove   Removes a member from a zone alias.
II. authUtil   Displays and sets the authentication configuration.
III. bladeDisable   Disables all user ports on a blade.
IV. bladeEnable   Enables all user ports on a blade.
V. cfgActvShow   Displays effective zone configuration information.
VI. cfgAdd   Adds a member to a zone configuration.
VII. cfgClear   Clears all zone configurations.
VIII. cfgCreate Creates a zone configuration.
IX. cfgDelete Deletes a zone configuration.
X. cfgDisable   Disables a zone configuration.
XI. cfgEnable   Enables a zone configuration.
XII. cfgRemove   Removes a member from a zone configuration.
XIII. cfgSave   Saves the zone configuration to nonvolatile memory.
XIV. cfgShow Displays zone configuration information.
XV. cfgSize   Displays zone and Admin Domain database size details.
XVI. chassisDisable   Disables all user ports in a chassis.
XVII. chassisDistribute   Distributes IP filter policies.
XVIII. chassisEnable   Enables all user ports in a chassis.
XIX. chassisName   Displays or sets the chassis name.
XX. chassisShow   Displays all field replaceable units (FRUs).
XXI. configDownload   Downloads configuration data to the system.
XXII. configList   Lists uploaded configuration files.
XXIII. configRemove   Deletes a saved configuration file.
XXIV. configShow   Displays system configuration settings.
XXV. configUpload   Uploads system configuration data to a file.
XXVI. configure   Changes switch configuration settings.
XXVII. configureChassis   Changes chassis-level system configuration settings.
XXVIII. cryptoCfg   Performs encryption configuration and management functions.
XXIX. errClear   Clears all error log messages for all switch instances
XXX. fabricName   Configures the fabric name parameter.
XXXI. fabricPrincipal   Sets the principal switch selection mode.
XXXII. fabricShow   Displays fabric membership information.
XXXIII. fabStatsShow   Displays fabric statistics.
XXXIV. fanDisable   Disables a fan unit.
XXXV. fanEnable   Enables a fan unit.
XXXVI. fanShow Displays fan status and speed.
XXXVII. fastBoot   Reboots the Control Processor CP
XXXVIII. firmwareCommit   Commits switch firmware.
XXXIX. firmwareDownload   Downloads firmware
XL. firmwareDownloadStatus   Displays the status of a firmware download.
XLI. firmwareKeyShow   Displays the public key used for signed firmware validation.
XLII. firmwareRestore   Restores the former active firmware image.
XLIII. firmwareShow   Displays the firmware version and download history.
XLIV. firmwareSync   Synchronizes the firmware from the active control processor (CP) to the standby CP.

XLV. nsAliasShow   Displays local Name Server (NS) information, with aliases.
XLVI. nsShow   Displays local Name Server (NS) information.
XLVII. nsZoneMember Displays the information on online devices zoned
XLVIII. nsZoneShow   Displays the zone names.
XLIX. passwd   Changes the password for a specified user.
L. passwdCfg   Manages the password policies.
LI. portAddress   Assigns the lower 16 bits of the Fibre Channel Port ID.
LII. portBeacon   Sets port beaconing mode.
LIII. portBufferCalc   Calculates the number of buffers required per port.
LIV. portBufferShow Displays the buffer usage information for a port group
LV. portCfg   Manages port configuration parameters for FC ports, VE_ports, and GbE/10GbE ports.
LVI. portCfgAutoDisable   Manages the port autodisable configuration.
LVII. portCfgCompress   Configures a port for compression.
LVIII. portCfgEncrypt Configures a port for encryption.
LIX. portEnable   Enables a port or a range of ports.
LX. portErrShow   Displays a port error summary.
LXI. portShow   Displays status and configuration parameters for ports
LXII. portZoneShow   Displays the enforced zone type of the F_Ports and FL_Ports
psShow   Displays power supply status.
LXIII. reboot   Reboots the control processor (CP).
LXIV. sfpShow Displays Small Form-factor Pluggable (SFP) transceiver information.
LXV. slotShow Displays the status of all slots in the system.
LXVI. supportFtp   Sets, clears, or displays support FTP parameters
LXVII. supportInfoClear   Clears all the default port statistic counters
LXVIII. supportSave   Saves RASLOG, TRACE, supportShow, core file, FFDC data
LXIX. supportShow   Displays switch information for debugging purposes.
LXX. topologyShow   Displays the unicast fabric topology.
LXXI. upTime   Displays length of time the system has been operational.
LXXII. version   Displays firmware version information.
LXXIII. wwn   Displays the world wide name (WWN)
LXXIV. wwnAddress   Binds an FC Port ID to a device WWN.
LXXV. zone   Performs specific zone operations.
LXXVI. zoneAdd Adds a member to the zone.
LXXVII. zoneCreate   Creates a zone.
LXXVIII. zoneDelete   Deletes a zone.
LXXIX. zoneHelp Displays a description of zoning commands.
LXXX. zoneObjectCopy   Copies a zone object.
LXXXI. zoneObjectExpunge   Expunges a zone object.
LXXXII. zoneObjectRename   Renames a zone object.
LXXXIII. zoneObjectReplace   Replaces zone members.
LXXXIV. zoneRemove   Removes a member from a zone.
LXXXV. zoneShow   Displays zone information.

What specifications you check for HDD Performance?

I. Access Time = Average Seek Time + Average Latency Time + Transfer Time
II. Access Time = Total time required to access a disk to read/write a block of data
III. The average seek time is fixed and is part of the disk specification
IV. The average latency time = ½ x 1/rotational speed
V. The transfer time = 1/ (number of sectors per track x rotational speed)
VI. Throughput = Transfer size/Transfer time
VII. Transfer time = RTT + Transfer size/Bandwidth
VIII. Total Seek time = Head Seek time + Rotational Latency + Transfer Time
IX. Number of IOPS a disk can achieve = 1/ (average latency in ms + average seek time for read or write in ms)
X. MHz per I/Ops = (Average CPU utilization × CPU rating in MHz × Number of cores) / (Number of I/O operations per second)
XI. Power consumed by a disk in Watts: (Number of Platters on the spindle)*(RPM) 2.8(Diameter in inches) 4.6

XII. Calculate Disk Capacity: Heads * Sectors/track * Sector size * NCyl (number of cylinders)
XIII. Seek Time =Time needed to move form the first to the last track
XIV. Latency =Time needed for one full revolution of the disk
XV. Transfer Time=Time needed for a block to pass under the head
XVI. Total Access Time =Sum of the above
XVII. HDD Capacity = Sides X Tracks X Sectors X Bytes/Sector
XVIII. Average rotational latency = 1/2 period of revolution.
Average time to locate sector = latency + head load time + head settling time + seek time

What is the impact of evolving Ethernet speed on SAN?

Converged data centers can be built using 10G Ethernet. 10-Gigabit Ethernet makes it possible for Ethernet to match the raw performance characteristics of Fiber Channel (FC) Storage Area Networks (SANs). Its now possible to build a single infrastructure for data networking, storage networking, and inter-processor communications and provide improved Total Cost of Ownership (TCO).Ethernet speeds available are 10 Gigabit Ethernet / 40 Gigabit Ethernet Also 25/50/100 Gigabit Ethernet is available. We can use Single Cable for Network and Storage.
It therefore simplifies infrastructure and reduces the number of cables and server adapters. Single network for everything makes virtualization and cloud deployments possible.

What is the current speed of Fiber Channel products?

Currently new products are using Gen 5 Fibre Channel at 16 Gbps Speed.

Gen 6 Fibre Channel is also available 32GFC and 128GFC speed.

Name some Gen 6 Products?

I. Brocade Gen 6 G620 switch
II. The Brocade X6 directors provide up to 384 32 Gbps line rate ports
III. QLogic 2700 Series Gen 6 (32 Gbps) Fibre Channel Adapters

Explain the use of Brocade UltraScale chassis connectivity?

Brocade UltraScale chassis connectivity provides dedicated 64 Gbps parallel Gen 5 Fibre Channel inter-chassis links (ICLs) to connect up to 10 Brocade DCX® 8510 Backbones,

Name some of the Flash Storage arrays?

EMC:
XtremeIO all-SSD array
DSSD D5 All-Flash Arrays
VMAX3

HDS:
All-flash Hitachi Virtual Storage Platform (VSP) F series
Enhanced models of the hybrid Hitachi VSP G series

NetApp:
EF540 all-flash array

Explain the main difference between FMD and SSD?

FMD

I. The flash module drive (FMD) uses advanced embedded multi core flash controller with multilayer cell (MLC) flash

II. Hitachi Accelerated Flash storage is a proprietary flash controller, a CPU with firmware that manages its multi-level cell (MLC) NAND flash-based storage module

Solid-state drive (SSD)
III. SSD uses single-level cell (SLC)
IV. Flash SSD is NAND-based memory to store data persistently.

V. Flash SSDs provide high performance, low latency storage, power saving because there is no spinning media.

Explain the technology behind EMC XtremIO?

Acccording to emc product release:

I. EXtremIO uses X-Brick that contains active/active controllers, a shared drive array enclosure (DAE) containing 25 enterprise multi-layer cell (eMLC) SSDs.

II. Metadata is written to cache and then to disk with Journal protected by distributing across all controllers.

Explain how VMware Site Recovery Manager works?

I. According to VMWARE, SRM is a DR workflow automation product
II. It is a plug-in for Virtual Center
III. It Collects all the VMs data in Protection Groups at primary site
IV. It executes an orderly Recovery Plan at DR site

What is SAN?

SAN (Storage Area Network) is a network specifically dedicated to the task of transporting data for storage and retrieval. SAN architectures are alternatives to storing data on disks directly attached to servers or storing data on Network Attached Storage (NAS) devices which are connected through general purpose networks.

Storage Area Networks are traditionally connected over Fibre Channel networks. Storage Area Networks have also been built using SCSI (Small Computer System Interface) technology. An Ethernet network which was dedicated solely to storage purposes would also quality as a SAN.

Internet Small Computer Systems Interface (iSCSI) is a SCSI variant which encapsulates SCSI data in TCP packets and transits them over IP networks. Fibre Channel over TCP/IP (FCIP) tunnels Fibre Channel over IP-based networks. The Internet Fibre Channel Protocol (iFCP) transports Fibre Channel Layer 4 FCP on IP networks.

Why you use SAN?

I. Provides Faster and effective disaster recovery
II. Provides HA redundancy for fault tolerance
III. Provides high-speed access
IV. Provides Security
V. Provides Scalability
VI. Provides Performance
VII. Provides Uptime

Think about what you already learn and remember easily?

Max IOPS an HBA Port can generate to any LUN = (Device Queue Depth per LUN * (1/ (Storage Latency in ms/1000)))

Calculation of the maximum Queue Depth: The queue depth is the number of I/O operations that can be run in parallel on a device.
Q = Storage Port Max Queue Depth / (I * L),
Q is the Queue Depth =Execution Throttle= Maximum Number of simultaneous I/O for each LUN any particular path to the Storage Port.
I is the number of initiators per Storage port
L is the quantity of LUNs in the storage group.

Max IOPS an HBA Port can generate to any LUN = (Device Queue Depth per LUN * (1/ (Storage Latency in ms/1000)))

FORMULA TO CALCULATE WORKLOAD BY IOPS

IOPS per drive = 1000 / (Seek Time + Latency) = IOPS

IOPS = 1/[AVERAGE LATENCY (IN SEC) + AVERAGE READ/WRITE SEEK TIME (IN SEC)]

A. Parity RAID 5 and 3: Disk IOPS = Read IOPS + 4*Write IOPS
B. Parity RAID 6: Disk IOPS = Read IOPS + 6*Write IOPS
C. Mirrored RAID: Disk IOPS = Read IOPS + 2*Write IOPS
D. RAID 10: 100% of the read IOPS for all the drives

        50% of the write IOPS for all the drives

A WWNN is a World Wide Node Name; used to uniquely identify a device in a Storage Area Network (SAN).

A WWPN is a World Wide Port Name; a unique identifier for each Fibre Channel port presented to a Storage Area Network (SAN).

WWN FORMATS

    I. Vendor Unique Code
   II. Product Code
  III. Product Type
  IV. Serial Number
   V. Port Number

WWPN FORMATS

    I. Section 1 – Format ID
   II. Section 2 – Vendor ID
  III. Section 3 - Vendor Unique

DOMAIN ID

Domain ID is a number that uniquely identifies a switch in a fabric.

By default, the valid range for an assigned domain ID list is from 1 to 239.

N_port id/FCID - is a 24 bit (3 byte) logical address assigned by a fabric.

It consists of 3 parts:

    I. Domain ID - each switch gets a Domain ID

II. Area ID - Group of ports
III. Port ID - end host connected to a switch

PHYSICAL STORAGE CAPACITY

I. 1 kilobyte (KB) = 1,000 bytes
II. 1 megabyte (MB) = 1,0002 bytes
III. 1 gigabyte (GB) = 1,0003 bytes
IV. 1 terabyte (TB) = 1,0004 bytes
V. 1 petabyte (PB) = 1,0005 bytes

LOGICAL STORAGE CAPACITY: BASE 2

I. 1 KB = 1,024 bytes
II. 1 MB = 1,024 KB or 1,0242 bytes
III. 1 GB = 1,024 MB or 1,0243 bytes
IV. 1 TB = 1,024 GB or 1,0244 bytes
V. 1 PB = 1,024 TB or 1,0245 bytes
VI. 1 block = 512 bytes

EFFECTIVE CAPACITY

The amount of data stored on a storage system, plus the amount of unused formatted capacity in that system.

The estimated effective capacity Ee:

$$Ee = D / (Fd / Ft).$$

D = the size of data already stored,
Fd be the formatted capacity used to store that data,
Ft be the total formatted capacity on the system

FIBRE CHANNEL LAYERS

Fibre channel Layer	Role
I. FC - 4	Defines how a Fibre Channel network will communicate with

		upper level applications (Audio / Video / IPI / SCSI / HIPPI / IP / 802.2)
II.	FC - 3	For advanced features: Striping, Hunt groups, Multicast
III.	FC - 2	Similar to the MAC (Media Access Layer) and defines how data from upper level applications is split into frames for transport over the lower layers (Framing Protocol / Flow Control)
IV.	FC - 1	Defines how frames are encoded and decoded for transport (Encode / Decode). The information transmitted over a fibre is encoded 8 bits at a time into a 10 bit Transmission Character.
V.	FC - 0	Defines the various media types that can carry Fibre Channel data (Single, Multimode, Copper: 133Mb, 266Mb, 531Mb, 1.06G, 2.12G & 4.25G)

FIBRE CHANNEL INDUSTRY ASSOCIATION ROADMAP

NAME	Line-Rate (GBaud)	Throughput (full duplex) (MBps)	Availability
A. 1GFC	1.0625	200	1997
B. 2GFC	2.125	400	2001
C. 4GFC	4.25	800	2004
D. 8GFC	8.5	1600	2005
E. 10GFC	10.52	2550	2008
F. 16GFC	14.025	3200	2011
G. 32GFC	28.05	6400	2014

FIBRE CHANNEL TECHNOLOGY OPTIONS NOMENCLATURE

100-SM-LL-L:

100	SM	LL	L
Speed (MB/sec)	Media	Transmitter	Distance

400 = 400 MB/sec | SM = Single Mode | LL = Longwave Laser | L = Long

200 = 200 MB/sec | M5 = Multimode (50um) | SL = Shortwave Laser w OFC | I = Intermediate

100 = 100 MB/sec | M6 = Multimode (62,5um) | SN = Shortwave Laser w/o OFC| S = Short

50 = 50 MB/sec | TV = Video Cable | LE = Longwave LED

| MI = Miniature Cable | EL = Electrical

| TP = Twisted Pair

VARIOUS CONNECTIVITY OPTIONS FOR LONG DISTANCE

	Dark Fibre	CWDM	DWDM	SONET/SDH	IP
Distance in KM	40	100	200	1000	Unlimited
Latency in us/km	5	5	Low	Medium	Variable
Bandwidth in Gbps	100	8 Channels, 2.5Gbps	100 Channels 40Gbps	OC-192 10Gbps	Variable
Cost	Low	Low	High	Medium	High

The required bandwidth is determined by measuring the average number of write operations and the average size of write operations over a period of time.

PID PORT IDENTIFIER FORMAT

PIDs are used by the routing and zoning services in Fibre Channel fabrics to identify ports in the network.
The PID is a 24-bit address built from three fields:
Domain,
Area_ID, and
AL_PA.

Each of the domain, area_ID, and AL_PA portions of the PID require eight bits in the address space.

IQN - ISCSI QUALIFIED NAME FORMAT

This iSCSI name type can be used by any organization which owns a domain name. This naming format is useful when an end user or service provider wishes to assign iSCSI names for targets and/or initiators.

```
            Org.        Subgroup Naming Authority
            Naming
Type  Date   Auth
+-++------+ +--------+ +------------------------------+
```

iSCSI Qualified Name (IQN) Format
The IQN format takes the form iqn.yyyy-mm.naming-authority: unique name, where:
yyyy-mm is the year and month when the naming authority was established.
Naming-authority is usually reverse syntax of the Internet domain name of the naming authority.
¦ unique name is any name you want to use, for example, the name of your host.

EUI - EXTENDED UNIQUE IDENTIFIER FORMAT

The IEEE defined 64-bit extended unique identifier (EUI-64) is a concatenation of a 24-bit Organizationally Unique Identifier (OUI) value administered by the IEEE Registration Authority and a 40-bit extension identifier assigned by the organization with that OUI assignment.

```
N
A  OUI    VSID
A
| - | ------- | ----------- |
```

The EUI format takes the form eui.16 hex digits.

SCSI STANDARDS

I. SCSI Standard	Burst Transfer
II. SCSI-1	5 MB/s
III. SCSI-2 (Fast SCSI, Fast Narrow)	10 MB/s
IV. SCSI-2 Fast Wide (Wide SCSI)	20 MB/s
V. SCSI-2 Differential Narrow	10 MB/s
VI. SCSI-2 Differential Wide	20 MB/s
VII. SCSI-3 Ultra Narrow (Fast-20)	20 MB/s
VIII. SCSI-3 Ultra Wide	40 MB/s
IX. SCSI-3 Wide Ultra2	80 MB/s
X. SCSI-3 Wide Ultra3	320 MB/s

PEAK ROLLING AVERAGE (PRA)

(PRA in MB/sec) x (cycle time seconds) = (Cumulative peak data change)

SAN 24-BIT PORT ADDRESS FIELDS

Bits 23-16	Bits 15-08	Bits 07-00
Domain Area	(Port)	Port (AL_PA)

SHARE RECOVERY TIERS

A. Tier 0: No off-site data – Possibly no recovery
B. Tier 1: Data backup with no hot site
C. Tier 2: Data backup with a hot site
D. Tier 3: Electronic vaulting
E. Tier 4: Point-in-time copies
F. Tier 5: Transaction integrity
G. Tier 6: Zero or near-Zero data loss
H. Tier 7: Highly automated, business integrated solution

Rebuild time of failed drive=Equalization Rate= Speed at which the hot spare is copied to replacement for a failed disk.

Time = ((Failed Hard Drive Capacity * Rebuild Rate) * Disk Type and Speed Adjustment) + (Failed Hard Drive Capacity * Equalization Rate)

RAID SPECIFICATIONS

RAID levels 3, 4, and 5 use the N+1 formula

Where the capacity of N number of devices will be used for data and the capacity of one of those devices will be dedicated to data protection, or Parity.

Usable + Parity = Raw Capacity

A. Raid 0 (Stripe): Minimum 2 disks, Excellent performance ,No redundancy

B. Raid 1 (Mirror): 2 Drives, High performance, High redundancy, very minimal penalty on write performance.

C. Raid 5 (Drives with Parity): Minimum 3 Drives, Good performance, Good redundancy, Good Price.

D. Raid 6 (Drives with Double Parity): Minimum 4 Drives, Additional fault tolerance.

E. Raid 10 (Mirror+Stripe) or 0+1 (Stripe+Mirror): Minimum 4 Drives, Stripe of mirrors, excellent redundancy, excellent performance. Usable capacity 50% of available disk drives

F. Raid 50 (Parity+Stripe): Minimum 6 Drives. Usable capacity is between 67% - 94%, fast, data redundancy.

G. Raid 60 (Double Parity+Stripe): Minimum 8 Drives, Usable capacity 50% - 88%, fast, extra data redundancy.

LUN ID

A SCSI address consists of a Target ID and a Logical Unit Number (LUN).

LUN ID is in hexadecimal value (00 - FF), which is mapped to the specified volume ID, Using a Decimal to hex converter, convert decimal number to hexadecimal as:

Device Address=the hexadecimal value that uniquely defines a physical I/O device on a channel path.

Decimal	Hex	Binary	Value
A. 000	00	00000000	
B. 001	01	00000001	
C. 002	02	00000010	
D. 003	03	00000011	
E. 004	04	00000100	
F. 005	05	00000101	
G. 006	06	00000110	
H. 007	07	00000111	
I. 008	08	00001000	
J. 009	09	00001001	
K. 010	0A	00001010	
L. 011	0B	00001011	
M. 012	0C	00001100	

N. 013	0D	00001101
O. 014	0E	00001110
P. 015	0F	00001111
Q. 016	10	00010000
R. 017	11	00010001
S. 018	12	00010010
T. 019	13	00010011
U. 020	14	00010100

HDD RELIABILITY

I. MTTF = Mean Time to Failure
II. MTTR = Mean Time to Repair
III. MTBF = Mean Time between Failures = MTTF + MTTR
IV. MTBF = (Total Time of all Parts run) / (Total number of failures)

SUPPORTED DISTANCES OF THE VARIOUS 62.5-MICRON CABLES

Speed	Length
1.0625 Gb	2 m (6.6 ft) min to 300 m (985 ft) max
2.125 Gb	2 m (6.6 ft) min to 150 m (492 ft) max
4 Gb	2 m (6.6 ft) min to 70 m (231 ft) max

BUFFER TO BUFFER CREDITS FOR LONG DISTANCE
A good rule of thumb is to use 1 BB credit for each kilometer (km) multiplied by the speed of the FC connection.

A. 1 Gigabit	0.5 Credit Per Kilometer
B. 2 Gigabit	1 Credit Per Kilometer

AVAILABILITY
System Availability: Availability = Uptime/ (Uptime + Downtime)
Availability Downtime
A. 99%   3.65 days a year.
B. 99.9% 8.76 hours a year.

C. 99.99%   52.56 minutes a year.
D. 99.999%   5.26 minutes a year.

LATENCY AND RPM

Latency time = (1/((Rotational Speed in RPM)/60)) * 0.5 * 1000 mili seconds

HDD Spindle RPM	Average rotational latency [ms]
I. 7,200	4.17
II. 10,000	3.00
III. 15,000	2.00

SAS

6Gb/s SAS, Double transfer rate to 6Gb/s, Up to 10m cable lengths

RETURN ON INVESTMENT (ROI)

ROI = (Net Profit / Cost of Investment) x 100

Total Cost of Ownership (TCO): It incorporates hardware and software costs, installation and license tracking, warranties and maintenance agreements.

RECOVERY

RPO= Maximum tolerable data loss (time since last backup)
RTO=Time needed from failure to recover and resume to business

The required Bandwidth=the required bandwidth is determined by measuring the average number of write operations and the average size of write operations over a period of time.

MODE CONDITIONING FIBER OPTIC CABLE

SUPPORTED DISTANCES OF THE VARIOUS 50-MICRON CABLES:

	Data rate/Link speed	M5 (OM2) cable	M5E (OM3) cable	M5F (OM4) cable
1	8 Gbps	50 m (164 ft.)	150 m (492 ft.)	190 m (623 ft.)
2	4 Gbps	150 m (492 ft.)	380 m (1 247 ft.)	400 m (1312 ft.)

Data-at-Rest encryption

Triple DES uses a "key bundle" which comprises three DES keys, K1, K2 and K3, each of 56 bits (excluding parity bits). The encryption algorithm is:

ciphertext = EK3(DK2(EK1(plaintext)))

Each triple encryption encrypts one block of 64 bits of data.

Non Technical/ Personal/ HR interview: Complimentary

Bottom Line Job interview?

Bottom-line: You will learn to answer any questions in such a way that you match your qualifications to the job requirements.

Interview Question?

Example response. Try to customize your answers to fit the requirements of the job you are interviewing for.

What are your greatest strengths?

I. **Articulate.**
II. **Achiever.**
III. **Organized.**
IV. **Intelligence.**
V. **Honesty.**
VI. **Team Player.**
VII. **Perfectionist.**
VIII. **Willingness.**
IX. **Enthusiasm.**
X. **Motivation.**
XI. **Confident.**
XII. **Healthy.**
XIII. **Likeability.**
XIV. **Positive Attitude.**
XV. **Sense of Humor.**
XVI. **Good Communication Skills.**
XVII. **Dedication.**
XVIII. **Constructive Criticism.**
XIX. **Honesty.**
XX. **Very Consistent.**
XXI. **Determination.**
XXII. **Ability to Get Things Done.**
XXIII. **Analytical Abilities.**
XXIV. **Problem Solving Skills.**
XXV. **Flexibility.**
XXVI. **Active in the Professional Societies.**
XXVII. **Prioritize.**
XXVIII. **Gain Knowledge by Reading Journals.**
XXIX. **Attention to details.**
XXX. **Vendor management skills.**
XXXI. **Excellent Project Management skills.**
XXXII. **Self-disciplined.**
XXXIII. **Self-reliant.**
XXXIV. **Self-starter.**

XXXV. Leadership.
XXXVI. Team-building.
XXXVII. Multitasking.
XXXVIII. Prioritization.
XXXIX. Time management.
XL. Can handle multiple projects and deadlines.
XLI. Thrives under pressure.
XLII. A great motivator.
XLIII. An amazing problem solver.
XLIV. Someone with extraordinary attention to detail.
XLV. Confident.
XLVI. Assertive.
XLVII. Persistent.
XLVIII. Reliable.
XLIX. Understand people.
L. Handle multiple priorities.
LI. Build rapport with strangers.

What are your greatest weaknesses?

I. I am working on My Management skills.
II. I feel I could do things on my own in a faster way without delegating it.
III. Currently I am learning to delegate work to staff members.
IV. I have a sense of urgency and I tend to push people to get work done.
V. I focus on details and think thru the process start to finish and sometimes miss out the overall picture, so I am improving my skills by laying a schedule to monitor overall progress.

Had you failed to do any work and regret?

I. I have No Regrets.
II. I am Moving on.

Where do you see yourself five years from now?

I. I am looking for a long-term commitment.
II. I see a great chance to perform and grow with the company.
III. I will continue to learn and take on additional responsibilities.
IV. If selected I will continue rise to any challenge, pursue all tasks to completion, and accomplish all goals in a timely manner.
V. I am sure if I will continue to do my work and achieve results more and more opportunities will open up for me.
VI. I will try to take the path of progression, and hope to progress upwards.
VII. In the long run I would like to move on from a technical position to a management position where I am able to smoothly manage, delegate and accomplish goals on time.
VIII. I want to Mentor and lead junior-to-mid level reporting analysts.
IX. I want to enhance my management experience in motivating and building strong teams.
X. I want to build and manage relationships at all levels in the organization.
XI. I want to get higher degree, new certification.

How Will You Achieve Your Goals?

Advancing skills by taking related classes, professional associations, participating in conferences, attending seminars, continuing my education.

Why are you leaving Your Current position?

    I. **More money**
    II. **Opportunity**
    III. **Responsibility**
    IV. **Growth**
    V. **Downsizing and upcoming merger, so I made a good, upward career move before my department came under the axe of the new owners.**

Why are you looking for a new job?

I have been promoted as far as I can go with my   current employer.
I'm looking for a new challenge that will give me the opportunity to use my skills to help me grow with the company.

Why should I hire you?

    I. **I know this business from ground up.**
    II. **I have Strong background in this Skill.**
    III. **Proven, solid experience and track record.**
    IV. **Highest level of commitment.**
    V. **Continuous education on current technical issues.**
    VI. **Direct experience in leading.**
    VII. **Hands-on experience.**
    VIII. **Excellent Project Management skills.**
    IX. **Demonstrated achievements.**
    X. **Knowledge base.**
    XI. **Communications skills.**
    XII. **Ability to analyze, diagnoses, suggests, and implements process changes.**
    XIII. **Strong customer service orientation.**
    XIV. **Detail oriented, strong analytical, organizational, and problem solving skill.**
    XV. **Ability to interact with all levels.**
    XVI. **Strong interpersonal, relationship management skills.**
    XVII. **Ability to work effectively with all levels, cultures, functions.**
    XVIII. **I am a good team player.**
    XIX. **Extensive Technical experience.**
    XX. **Understanding of Business.**
    XXI. **Result and customer-oriented.**
    XXII. **Strong communication skills.**
    XXIII. **Good Project and Resource management skills.**
    XXIV. **Exceptional interpersonal and customer service skills.**
    XXV. **Strong analytical, evaluative, problem-solving abilities.**
    XXVI. **Good management and planning skills.**
    XXVII. **Good Time Management skills.**

XXVIII. Ability to work independently.
XXIX. I've been very carefully looking for the jobs.
XXX. I can bring XX years of experience.
XXXI. That, along with my flexibility and organizational skills, makes me a perfect match for this position.
XXXII. I see some challenges ahead of me here, and that's what I thrive on.
XXXIII. I have all the qualifications that you need, and you have an opportunity that I want. It's a 100% Fit.

Aren' t you overqualified for this position?

I. In My opinion in the current economy and the volatile job market overqualified is a relative term.
II. My experience and qualifications make me do the job right.
III. I am interested in a long term relationship with my employer.
IV. As you can see my skills match perfectly.
V. Please see my longevity with previous employers.
VI. I am the perfect candidate for the position.
VII. What else can I do to convince you that I am the best candidate? There will be positive benefits due to this.
Since I have strong experience in this ABC skill I will start to contribute quickly. I have all the training and experience needed to do this job. There's just no substitute for hands on experience.

Describe a Typical Work Week?

I. Meeting every morning to evaluate current issues.
II. Check emails, voice messages.
III. Project team meeting.
IV. Prioritize issues.
V. Design, configure, implement, maintain, and support.
Perform architectural design. Review and analysis of business reports.
VI. Conduct weekly staff meetings.
VII. Support of strategic business initiatives.
VIII. Any duties as assigned. Implementation.
IX. Monitor and analyze reports.
Routine maintenance and upgrades.
X. Technical support.
XI. Deploy and maintain.
XII. Provide day-to-day support as required.
Work with customers and clients.
XIII. Documentation.
XIV. Standard operating procedures.
XV. Tactical planning.
XVI. Determine and recommend.
XVII. Plan and coordinate the evaluation.
XVIII. Effective implementation of technology solutions.
XIX. To meet the business objectives.
XX. Participation in budget matters.
XXI. Readings to Keep Abreast Of Current Trends and Developments in the Field.

Are You Willing to Travel?

I. For the right opportunity I am open to travel.
II. I'm open to opportunities so if it involves relocation I would consider it.

Describe the pace at which you work?

I. I work at a consistent and steady pace.
II. I try to complete work in advance of the deadline.
III. I am able to manage multiple projects simultaneously.
IV. I am flexible with my work speed and try to conclude my projects on time.
V. So far I have achieved all my targets
VI. I meet or exceeded my goals.

How Did You Handle Challenges?

I. Whenever the project got out of track I Managed to get the project schedules back on the track.
II. Whenever there was an issue I had researched the issues and found the solutions.
III. We were able to successfully troubleshoot the issues and solve the problems, within a very short period of time.

How do you handle pressure? Stressful situations?

I. In personal life I manage stress by going to a health club.
II. I remain calm in crisis.
III. I can work calmly with many supervisors at the same time.
IV. I use the work stress and pressure in a constructive manner.
V. I use pressure to stay focused, motivated and productive.
VI. I like working in a challenging environment.
VII. By Prioritizing.
VIII. Use time management
IX. Use problem-solving
X. Use decision-making skills to reduce stress.
XI. Making a "to-do" list.
XII. Site stress-reducing techniques such as stretching and taking a break.
XIII. Asked for assistance when overwhelmed.

How Many Hours Do You Work?

I enjoy solving problems and work as much as necessary to get the job done.
The Norm is 40 hour week.

Why are you the best person for the job?

I. It's a perfect fit as you need someone like me who can produce results that you need, and my background and experience are proof.
II. As you can see in My resume I've held a lot of similar positions like this one, and hence I am a perfect fit as all those experiences will help me here.
III. I believe this is a good place to work and it will help me excel.

What are you looking for in a position?

I. **I'm looking for an opportunity where I may be able to apply my skills and significantly contribute to the growth of the company while helping create some advancement and more opportunities for myself.**
II. **It seems this organization will appreciate my contributions and reward my efforts appropriately to keep me motivated.**
III. **I am looking for job satisfaction and the total compensation package to meet My Worth that will allow me to make enough money to support my lifestyle.**

What do you know about our organization?

I. **This is an exciting place to work and it fits my career goals.**
II. **This company has an impressive   growth.**
III. **I think it would be rewarding to be a part of such a company.**

What are your short term goals?

I'd like to find a position that is a good fit and where I can contribute and satisfy my professional desires.

What Salary are you looking for?

I. **Please provide me the information about the job and the responsibilities involved before we can begin to discuss salary.**
II. **Please give me an idea of the range you may have budgeted for this position.**
III. **It seems my skills meet your highest standards so I would expect a salary at the highest end of your budget.**
IV. **I believe someone with my experience should get between A and B.**
V. **Currently I am interested in talking more about what the position can offer my career.**
VI. **I am flexible but, I'd like to learn more about the position and your staffing needs.**
VII. **I am very interested in finding the right opportunity and will be open to any fair offer you may have.**

Tell me more about yourself.

I. **I'm an experienced professional with extensive knowledge.**
II. **Information tools and techniques.**
III. **My Education.**
IV. **A prominent career change.**
V. **Personal and professional values.**
VI. **Personal data.**
VII. **Hobbies.**
VIII. **Interests.**
IX. **Describe each position.**
X. **Overall growth.**

XI. **Career destination.**

Why did you leave your previous job?

I. **Relocation.**
II. **Ambition for growth.**
III. **This new opportunity is a better fit for my skills and/or career ambitions.**
IV. **To advance my career and get a position that allows me to grow.**
V. **I was in an unfortunate situation of having been downsized.**
VI. **I'm looking for a change of direction.**
VII. **I want to visit different part of the country I'm looking to relocate.**
VIII. **I am looking to move up with more scope for progression.**

What relevant experience do you have?

I have these XYZ related experience.
I have these skills that can apply to internal management positions et al.

If your previous co-workers were here, what would they say about you?

Hard worker, most reliable, creative problem-solver, Flexible, Helping

Where else have you applied?

I am seriously looking and keeping my options open.

What motivates you to do a good job?

Recognition for a job well done.

Are you good at working in a team?

Yes.

Has anything ever irritated you about people you've worked with?

I've always got on just fine with all my co-workers.

Is there anyone you just could not work with?

No.

Tell me about any issues you've had with a previous boss.

I never had any issues with my boss.

Do you have any questions?

Please explain the benefits and bonus.
How soon could I start, if I were offered the job?

Why did you choose this career?

    I.   **Life style.**
   II.   **Passion.**
  III.   **Desire.**
  IV.   **Interesting.**
   V.   **Challenging.**
  VI.   **Pays Well.**
 VII.   **Demand.**

What did you learn from your last job experience?

I gained experience that's directly related to this job.

Why is there a gap in your resume?

Because of Personal and family reasons I was unable to work for some time.
   I.   **Unemployed.**
  II.   **Job hunt.**
 III.   **Layoffs.**

How do you keep current and informed about your job and the industries that you have worked in?

  I. **I pride myself on my ability to stay on top of what is happening in the industry.**
 II. **I do a lot of reading.**
III. **I belong to a couple of professional organizations.**
 IV. **I have a strong network with colleagues.**
  V. **I take classes and seminars.**
 VI. **I have started and participated in many technical blogs.**

Tell me about a time when you had to plan and coordinate a project from start to finish?

   I. **I headed up a project which involved customer service personnel and technicians.**
  II. **I organized a meeting and got everyone together.**
 III. **I drew up a plan, using all best of the ideas.**
  IV. **I organized teams.**
   V. **We had a deadline to meet, so I did periodic checks with various teams involved.**
  VI. **After four weeks, we were exceeding expectations.**
 VII. **We were able to begin implementation of the plan.**
VIII. **It was a great team effort, and a big success.**
  IX. **I was commended by management for my managing capacity.**

What kinds of people do you have difficulties working with?

  I. **I have worked in very diverse teams.**
 II. **Diversity means differences and similarities with men and women from very diverse backgrounds and culture. It helps us grow as a human being.**
III. **The only difficulty was related to work related dishonesty by a person.**
 IV. **He was taking credit for all the work our team accomplished.**

What do you want to be in 5 years?

I hope to develop my management skills by managing a small staff.

Explain an Ideal career for you?

  I. **I would like to stay in a field of ABC.**
 II. **I have been good at ABC.**
III. **I look forward to ABC.**

What are your job responsibilities?

I would expect expanded responsibilities that could make use of my other skills.

What is your dream job?

Includes all of the responsibilities and duties you are trying to fill.

I also thrive in the fast changing environment where there is business growth.

What skills you have?

I was very pleased to develop the A, B, C skills that you are seeking.

What sets you apart?

    I. **Once I am committed to a job or project I take it with tremendous intensity.**
    II. **I want to learn everything I can.**
    III. **I am very competitive and like to excel at everything I do.**

If the project not gone as planned what action you will take?

Backup and identify precautions.

What you do if you are unable to meet deadlines?

    I. **Negotiate.**
    II. **Discussion.**
    III. **Restructure.**
    IV. **Redefine Optimum goal.**
    V. **Show a price structure.**

Interpersonal skill?

    I. **I had to learn to say no.**
    II. **Helpful to other staff.**
    III. **Help in return.**

Improve?

In any job I hold I can usually find inefficiencies in a process, come up with a solution.

What do you feel has been your greatest work-related accomplishment?

    I. **Implemented an idea to reduce expenses, raised revenues.**
    II. **Solved real problems.**
    III. **Enhanced department's reputation.**

Have you ever had to discipline a problem employee? If so, how did you handle it?

Yes.

I did it using:

    I. **Problem-solving skills**
    II. **Listening skills, and**
    III. **Coaching skills**

Why do you want this position?

    I. **I always wanted the opportunity to work with a company that leads the industry in innovative products.**
    II. **My qualifications and goals complement the company's mission, vision and values.**
    III. **I will be able to apply and expand on the knowledge and experience, and will be able to increase my contributions and value to the company through new responsibilities.**

Why are you the best person for this job?

    I. **I have extensive experience in XYZ (Skill they are looking for)**
    II. **I'm a fast learner.**
    III. **I adapt quickly to change.**
    IV. **I will hit the ground running.**
    V. **I'm dedicated and enthusiastic.**
    VI. **I'm an outstanding performer.**
    VII. **I may be lacking in this specific experience but I'm a fast learner and I'll work harder.**

What about Technical writing?

    I. **I can convert any complex technical information into simple, easy form.**
    II. **I can write reports to achieve maximum results.**

How versatile you are? Can you do other works?

I am flexible and can adapt to any changing situations.

How do you manage time?

    I. **I am very process oriented and I use a systematic approach to achieve more in very less time.**
    II. **I effectively eliminate much paperwork.**

How do you handle Conflicts?

    I. **I am very tactful;**
    II. **I avoid arguments and frictions and**
    III. **I establish trust and mutual understanding.**

What kind of supervisory skills you have?

I. I make sure that everyone understands their responsibilities.
II. I try to be realistic in setting the expectations and try to balance the work among all.

Any Bad Situation you could not solve?

I've never yet come across any situation that couldn't be resolved by a determined, constructive effort.

Anything else you want to say?

I. I am excited and enthusiastic about this opportunity
II. I am looking forward to working with you.

About the Author: Kumar has specialized in designing and implementing Storage Area Network (SAN) solutions. His main areas of interest lie in Storage Networking, Virtualization and Performance tuning.

Reference, Copyright & Trademark Acknowledgement Statements:

Disclaimer of Warranty: